ALASTAIR COOK

ENGLAND CRICKETER

MR VIVEK KUMAR PANDEY SHAMBHUNATH

ISBN 979-888591011-8

Disclaimer : During Writing This Book No character & No religious , No Relation Members Are Harmed. It's Only For Study & Entertainment Purpose. Do Not Take Seriously. Short Biopic Written In This Book Written By Mr Vivek Kumar Pandey.

Contents

Foreword *vii*

Preface *ix*

1. Alastair Cook 1

2. England Cricket Team 17

3. History Of The England Cricket 34

4. What Is Cricket ? 48

Foreword

Short biography of Alastair Cook and about life.During writing this book No character & No religious are harmed written by Mr Vivek Kumar Pandey. winner youngest writer award 1st rank in india 2020.He is only one writer can publish 870+ own book that was greatest successfull in his life.This All Credit Goes To My Super Hero Daddy.

Preface

Author biography in English :MY NAME IS VIVEK KUMAR PANDEY . I WAS BORN IN 30 SEP 2002,I AM FROM SURAT GUJARAT INDIA.MY DREAM WAS TO BE GOOD WRITERS ,MY FAMILY SUPPORTED ME TO SUCCESSFUL AND I CAN DO IT MY SELF.How do I write? That is a question, I believe, that can be honestly answered by me."CELEBRATING YOUNGEST WRITER AWARD WINNER IN GUJARAT 1ST RANK" MR PANDEY JI . I may think I did a good job writing something . The reader is the one who decides the quality of my writing. I do find writing to be natural to me and therefore find it to be a real challenge. My trick as a challenged writer is to do the best I can and know that I am happy with the final outcome. It may take a while to do my best and there may be quite a few problems I run into along the way.

I am not a greedy person those who are thinking about me and my self I never tried it anyone people suffering from sadness ,I trying to get promoted people suffering from happiness and joy in your Life Time. Now in current situation in India and also world people are unemployed and have no many but our indian governor help to people to get free food from ration card , i also take part in leadership team ,i am Motivational speaker , Film script writer. There was my two dream firstly writer and secondly actor & also my own film is upcoming soon i done almost completely completed script for my film .I AM GOING TO SAY WORD OF HEART TOUCH OUT PLEASE READ IT" , firstly i thanks my father he supports me in this field they always getting inspired me by own his words and behavior ,they always said that he was a biggest person in the world in future and also they purchase fruit and chocolate for me in anytime & anyway , firstly my father buy him then call me Vivek you want a chocolate i will say yes papa but how many tell me ,papa: you tell me how much i buy him i told 1 or 2 chocolate but my father purchase whole the boxes of chocolate and they get suprised me. MY FATHER WAS BORN IN " 20 SEPTEMBER" 1971 IN INDIA.

1) MY FATHER FAVORITE CLOTHES IS KURTA PAIJMA AND ALSO STYLES SHOE

2) FAVORITE SINGER IS KISHORE DA

3) FAVORITE STATE GUJARAT AND KOLKATA , HIS VILLAGE IN BIHAR

4) FAVORITE COLOR BLACK AND WHITE

THEY ALSO LOVE cricket like IPL and one day t-20 .they also like watching a News daily and heard the song daily ,they also interested in tik tok video but in current time tik tok is banned in india but also few videos are in you tube. In lockdown time my family and me very enjoy day daily. my father play daily ludo with his sister and son, daughter.they always loved tea and coffee anytime call me "I . I make it tea for my father but some reason after the April to june they are suffering from fever and cough , weakness on 6 June 2020 my father death. they not told me say bye bye his life. After death of 6 June on 10 june my mom and dad anniversary.but my father is Best in the world they can do anything for me please take care of father and respect it of your parents.

CHAPTER ONE

Alastair Cook

- Alastair Cook

1. Disclaimer : During Writing This Book No character & No religious , No Relation Members Are Harmed. It's Only For Study & Entertainment Purpose. Do Not Take Seriously. Short Biopic Written In This Book Written By Mr Vivek Kumar Pandey.

Alastair Cook (born 25 December 1984) is an English cricketer who plays for County Cricket Club, and played for England in all international formats until retiring in 2018. A former captain of the England Test and One-Day International (ODI) teams, he is the fifth-highest Test run scorer of all time and holds a number of English and international records.

Cook is England's second most-capped Test player and has captained the English team in 59 Tests, as well as in 69 ODIs. He is the leading run-scorer in Test matches for England, and the youngest player to score 12,000 Test runs (the sixth overall, and the only Englishman). Cook has scored a record 33 Test centuries for England and is the first England player to win 50 Test matches. A left-handed opening batsman (the highest-scoring left-hander in Tests), he normally fields at first slip.

Cook played for Essex's Academy and made his debut for the first XI in 2003. He played in several of England's youth teams from 2000 until his call up to the Test side in 2006. While touring in the West Indies with the ECB National Academy, Cook was called up to the England national team in India as a last-minute replacement for Marcus Trescothick and debuted, aged 21, with a century. He went on to score 1,000 runs in his maiden year and made centuries in his first Test matches against India, Pakistan, the West Indies and Bangladesh. Cook played a pivotal role in England winning the 2009

Ashes series, and, after deputising as Test captain in 2010 and then taking ODI captaincy full-time, in retaining the Ashes in 2010-11.

He was appointed captain of the Test team after Andrew Strauss's retirement on 29 August 2012. Cook captained England to its first Test series victory in India since 1984–85. During the tour he became the first captain to score a century in each of his first five Tests in charge. On 30 May 2015, Cook became the leading run-scorer in Test matches for England, surpassing Graham Gooch (8900).

After England's 2016 tour of Bangladesh and India, he stepped down as Test captain. Cook was appointed MBE in 2011 and promoted to CBE in 2016 for services to cricket. On 24 May 2018 during the first Test against Pakistan, Cook equalled Allan Border's record for appearing in the greatest number of consecutive Test matches, with 153, surpassing it a week later in the second Test at Headingley. On 3 September 2018, Cook announced that his twelve-year international career would end at the conclusion of the series against India on 11 September 2018. In the 2019 New Year Honours, Cook was appointed a Knight Bachelor for services to cricket.

On the occasion of England's 1000th Test in August 2018, he was named in the country's greatest Test XI by the ECB.

- *Alastair Cook life and education*

Cook was born in Gloucester; his mother Stephanie is a teacher from Swansea,while his father Graham worked as a telecommunications engineer and enjoyed village cricket. Cook is a keen musician: by the age of eight he was learning the clarinet and became a boarding pupil at St Paul's Cathedral School in London, an independent school connected to the cathedral, as a chorister, with a rigorous schedule of rehearsals. Cook later claimed the amount of focus and concentration required to keep practising while undergoing regular school hours helped with his batting.

When he was a boy, his family lived in Wickham Bishops, a village near Witham in central Essex. During his summer holidays, Cook played cricket for nearby Maldon Cricket Club, and by the age of 11 he was already playing in the adult Third XI. He played sporadically for Maldon over seven years, with an average of 168 in his final year. He is now an honorary life member of the club.

Aged 13, Cook's musical flair led to him to becoming a boarding pupil at Bedford School, an independent school for boys in the county town of

Bedford.He sang, played the clarinet to grade eight and learned to play piano and saxophone. Music was soon eclipsed when the Marylebone Cricket Club (MCC) came to play against the Bedford School XI. The visiting side were a man short and drafted the 14-year-old new boy to play against his school, and Cook scored a century.

Over the next four years, he hit 17 centuries and two double-hundreds to total 4,396 runs at an average of 87.90, captaining the cricket team in his final year under coach Jeremy 'Boris' Farrell, as well as being President of the Music Society. He also gained three A-Levels and nine GCSEs. In his final year at Bedford in 2003, he scored 1,287 runs for the school, including two unbeaten double-hundreds, averaging 160.87 to take the school record. After his international success, Cook returned for an Old Boys' match at Bedford in 2008, playing for the Head Master's Ultimate XI. Later on, Cook spent two years at Alleyn's School as a PE teacher.

- *Cook batting in 2005*

Having been a member of the Essex Academy since the age of 16, Cook was given his first-class debut for Essex against Nottinghamshire County Cricket Club on leaving school at the end of the 2003 season; put in to field he aided the first dismissal with a catch before scoring just 13 runs in his first innings but pushing Essex to a nine wicket victory with 69 not out in the second. Despite Essex's relegation being assured, Cook still battled away with an opening stand of 122 opposite Will Jefferson in the second innings of his second match, against Warwickshire.In the six innings in which he participated he quickly racked up three half centuries at an average of 47.80.Having secured his place as opener in the county team, he made his maiden first-class century against Leicestershire in May 2004 with 126 opposite Jefferson's 128 for a 265 opening stand, Essex's third-highest but the team failed to secure promotion.

His exploits in his single season gained enough attention for him to be brought in as opening batsman for the MCC in 2005 season's opener against County Champions Warwickshire. With a century in the first innings and 97 in the second, Cook helped secure victory in a match destined for a draw. The season opener would not be Cook's only highlight for the year: as the Ashes approached, Australia were touring the counties and in a two-day match (which did not count towards his first-class statistics) Cook scored a double century and went on to take the first wicket of Justin Langer with a catch in the drawn match days after being awarded PCA Young Cricketer of the Year.

A further highlight of the season saw Cook help Essex to achieve one of Durham's two defeats of the season, scoring 107 of Essex's 245 before taking his maiden first-class wicket, followed by another two, with his off-spin. Cook played in every first-class match for Essex and also helped them clinch the Totesport League Title for the first time in 20 years. The end of the season saw Cook finish with an average of 48.03 in the County Championship, hitting four centuries.

- *Alastair Cook playing for Essex in 2010*

After his England call up, Cook's appearances at Essex significantly reduced. In the County Championship he appeared in only three matches, making two hundreds and another two fifties in his five innings, topping the season averages with an inflated 141.3.

Similarly in the Cheltenham & Gloucester Trophy he appeared only three times and again topped the batting averages, only being out once with a top score of 91 and average of 148. He scored less favourably in his one Twenty20 Cup appearance, scoring only nine runs.In the 2007 season, for Essex alone his first-class average was only 58.8 from three appearances, making two hundreds but countering this with one duck and he made a similar century/duck appearance in the (formerly C&G) Friends Provident Trophy during his 5 matches averaging 38.4.

The back to back Totesport/Pro40 champions saw Cook make only one appearance in that competition, scoring 81 not out, before being relegated. They won Division Two and were promoted the following season, though Cook only provided 11 runs in one innings during the tournament.Despite his international commitments Cook managed to participate in at least one match of each tournament averaging 36.16 in three County Championship matches and 15 in his one Twenty20 match. Given time off the South Africa One-Day series, Cook fared better in the FP Trophy with 45.3 from 3 matches including contributing the second-highest in the final at Lord's to seal the trophy.

The 2009 English season featured an early Test series against the West Indies where, despite being in the Test team, Cook joined Essex in a tour match. He scored 76 not out in the second innings before the match was rained off, stopping Essex pressing for victory. Before the Test series he helped Essex force the follow on against Kent in the County Championship but faltered with his team, scoring only 4 in the second innings to lose by 192 runs.

After the Test series, Cook was omitted from the one day side leaving him free to play for Essex. He joined them in their bid to defend their Friends Provident Trophy matching Varun Chopra's 65 in a 124 run partnership against Lancashire to gain a place in the semi-final.He and his team could not recreate the same form for the semi-final, at the same location against the same team three days later, after being caught from a running catch by Sajid Mahmood, seeing the team lose by 67 runs.

Having been knocked out of the FP Trophy, the team turned to the Twenty20 Cup. Making only his fourth appearance in the tournament since 2005, Cook hit 80 off 56 balls in a match against Kent that was rained off. While his England partner Bopara scored 45 against Sussex, Cook only scored one but made up for this with a 60 run partnership with Bopara days later to put Essex top of the table. Despite averaging 49 from these four games, Cook felt he was a long way from the international squad. In his last performance before joining the Ashes squad, Cook scored a 57 ball century, and batted throughout the whole innings as they beat Surrey, but without Cook and Bopara, the team were knocked out after two successive losses.

- *Alastair Cook batting in 2019*

When Cook retired from international cricket in 2018, he stated that he would continue to play for Essex, signing a three-year contract with them. In the 2019 County Championship season Cook helped Essex to win the title In August 2020, during the 2020 Bob Willis Trophy, Cook scored his 24,000th run in first-class cricket.

- *Alastair Cook youth*

Cook had his first taste of international cricket playing the U15 World Cup in 2000. Three years later Cook was called up to the England Under-19 team for their tour of South Africa. After it was decided Samit Patel had enough responsibility batting and bowling, Cook was appointed captain of the team the following year, 2004. His first call of duty was the U19 World Cup in the West Indies where he guided England through the group stages and on past the Super League stage, including an unbeaten century-each partnership with Patel against New Zealand, and continued a 100% win record with 87 over eventual winners Pakistan before falling short in the semi-final against the West Indies. He went on from there to captain them in a U19 Test win over Bangladesh before taking the One-Day series too. His career with the Under 19 team was cut short when Kevin Pietersen was called up to replace Andrew Flintoff in the main team, leaving a spot in England A tour of Sri Lanka for Cook.

After the 2005 domestic season he was part of the intake for the ECB National Academy, but this was interrupted as he flew to Pakistan to cover the squad for Michael Vaughan's knee injury.After not being used in the first XI he travelled back with the Academy to the West Indies in the new year scoring 101 in a two-day match against Antigua before youth cricket came to an abrupt halt for Cook.

- *Alastair Cook 2006: India and Sri Lanka*

Cook was included in the ECB National Academy in the winter of 2005–06. The Academy's tour of the West Indies was cut short on 24 February for Cook who only appeared in the first innings, scoring only 6, before being called up, alongside James Anderson and Owais Shah, to the England tour of India[66] to replace captain Michael Vaughan, who was suffering from a knee injury, and opener Marcus Trescothick, who was suffering from stress.

Unlike Shah and Anderson, Cook was welcomed straight into the England XI and made his Test debut aged 21, days after he had flown in from the West Indies. He made an instant impact, opening with Andrew Strauss and scoring a half century in the first innings before being bowled just before tea on the first day for 60 runs from 160 balls being the second top scorer after 134 from Paul Collingwood.

The second innings would prove to cement him in cricket history as he went on to score 104 not out before England declared, making him the sixteenth Englishman to score a century on his debut Test and an even more exclusive list of five to score 100 and 50 in their first Test. His hundred was also the 3,000th century in Test cricket. Despite being known for a patient style of play, an impending declaration forced Cook to play quickly to bring up the century; regardless, the match was drawn. After a mediocre outing in the losing second Test, scoring 17 and 2, he missed the Third Test due to a stomach illness and was omitted from the one-day series.

Returning home, Cook was again selected for the first XI during Sri Lanka's tour. For his debut match at Lord's, Cook was shuffled down to third to make way for the returning Trescothick. However, he still walked to the crease alongside his teammate as Strauss fell at the stroke of lunch. Cook and Trescothick put on 127 in their partnership as Trescothick made a century while Cook later stumbled just before at 89. there was no second innings as England enforced the follow-on but were one wicket away from victory, with Cook being targeted among others for two significant dropped catches. Cook's first taste of victory came in the second Test, guiding the team past the target of 78 in the second innings with an unbeaten 34 alongside Andrew Flintoff furthering the reputation of his calm, meticulous style of play against the dangerous spin of Muttiah Muralitharan who took 4–29. Although not initially selected for the one-day series, Cook made his limited overs debut in the fourth match scoring 39 from 38 balls in a bright spot of an otherwise dour England performance hampered by injuries.

- *Alastair Cook 2006: Pakistan and Australia*

At the start of the following series against Pakistan, Cook recorded his second Test century, gaining him a spot on the boards at Lord's alongside Ian Bell and Collingwood.He and Bell both recorded back to back centuries by the following Test at Old Trafford as well as Cook scoring his then-career best 127 in an innings defeat over Pakistan. In what now seemed a pattern, Cook's century came up while partnering with Collingwood as with his previous two. In the controversial forfeited Test, sometimes called Ovalgate, Cook contributed a first innings top score of 40 and second best 83 before Pakistan refused to return to the field. This score secured Cook's tally of runs, 403, as the second-highest scorer for England and third overall in the series. Once again Cook was overlooked in the one day series. At the end of the season he was again awarded the Young Player of the Year award as well as being shortlisted for ICC Emerging Player of the Year.

As well as the one day series against Pakistan, Cook was overlooked for the 2006 Champions Trophy squad. However, he was named for the 2006–07 Ashes series touring party and when Trescothick pulled out once again due to stress, Cook re-earned a spot as an opener for the foreseeable future. In the disastrous 5 Test whitewash, Cook failed to impress in the first two Tests, but during a two-day warm-up he retired with a century and afterwards remained adamant that he and England would make a turn around in the series.

With England desperately chasing 577 runs, or a draw to not lose the Ashes, Cook stayed at the crease for over six hours, lasting almost all of the fourth day to earn his maiden Ashes century (119) before being caught behind off Glenn McGrath just shy of three overs before the close of play. This was his fourth Test century before turning 22, no England player had scored more than two by the same age.With only three other batsmen scoring double figures, England lost the Test and the Ashes and despite only having an average of 27.6 runs, Cook scored one of only three English centuries on the tour and also on 28 December 2006 in Melbourne, Cook scored his thousandth Test run, the second cricketer to do this in their maiden year, after Mark Taylor.

- *Alastair Cook in T20*

After being omitted for the Twenty20 International against Australia and the 2007 World Cup, Cook found himself once again in favour for the home series against West Indies. Starting at Lord's, Cook found himself among four centurions in the opening innings with Collingwood opposite him once again, being one of only five Englishmen to hit as many centuries in 15 Tests and recorded another half century in the following innings to win his first Man of The Match award. After another half century in the second Test, Cook recorded another half century/century combination in the two innings at Old Trafford, his first innings sixty equating to the team's win margin. Cook was selected for his first Twenty20 International against the West Indies, in a losing effort where he scored 15 runs from 16 balls. This was followed by a disappointing one-day series for Cook, and England, who averaged 22 in 3 matches.

The following home series against India saw Cook continue his fine Test form despite England not winning a Test. He was the third-highest scoring Englishman with an average of 37. In the first Test, Cook made scores of 36 and 17 as the match ended in a draw. During the first day of the second Test at Trent Bridge, Cook became the youngest English player to rack up 1,500 Test runs eclipsing the record held by David Gower. In the first innings of the third Test, Cook made his biggest score of the series, 61 and followed this up with 43 in the second innings to help England secure a draw. Cook played in six of the seven ensuing one-day matches, scoring his maiden ODI century in the first match alongside Ian Bell's 126 not out guiding England to a 104 win victory that propped up England's first one-day series victory since 2005. After two ducks, Cook was dropped in the final, decisive match.

After being omitted from the World Twenty20 Cook rejoined England in Sri Lanka making an outstanding contribution in both forms of the game. Starting with another ODI series victory, Cook battled with a stomach virus to top score 47 in a losing match and went on to be the second-highest scoring batsmen in the series behind Chamara Silva with 155. Cook also picked up his first ODI Man of The Match award in the fourth game after scoring 80 to help England win by five wickets. After an unsuccessful first Test, Cook went on to be the top scoring Test batsmen for England too, scoring two half centuries in the second Test and 118 in the third match, at an average of 46. Up until this tour, Cook had held a strange record of having more Test centuries than half centuries but this century marked his last until March 2009 and Cook came under increasing criticism for his lack of ability to convert fifties to hundreds at the top of the order, yet maintained an average in the low forties.

- *Alastair Cook 2008: New Zealand, South Africa and India*

England's tour of the antipodes continued with the tour of New Zealand and Cook made a great start in the warm up matches, making a half century followed by an unbeaten 138 the following day in limited overs matches. His style was still considered too slow for the following two Twenty20 Internationals and he failed to continue his form in the first ODI where he fell for 11 as part of an England collapse. The second match saw a similar collapse by England where Cook's 52 was the only real contribution until he was run out by fellow Essexian Ravi Bopara. The fourth one-day match saw Cook and Phil Mustard prop up the innings with an opening stand of 158 before both being dismissed in successive balls, leading to a tied match.

Although normally known for his slow but focussed repose with the bat, the first Test against New Zealand gave Cook a chance making three sharp catches in the first innings and mirroring his efforts with three even more spectacular catches in the second innings, the first two off Ryan Sidebottom who then went on to make a hat-trick with a final LBW, the match itself saw England collapse in the second innings for 110 with Cook being the only other player besides Ian Bell to make it into double figures. Incidentally, Cook's other catch in the second innings was also off Sidebottom to dismiss New Zealand captain Daniel Vettori, a feat the pair reproduced in the second innings of the second Test and again in the first innings of the third Test. His batting meanwhile began its long road of decline scoring no more than sixty in the two Tests and falling for only two runs in the final match, though in the second Test he did secure another English record being the youngest Englishman at just over 23 years, to score 2,000 Test runs – again eclipsing Gower; two days later he recorded his first Test six after 2047 runs, including 233 boundaries, after an accidental top edge and ruined his chances of beating Vijay Manjrekar's 2,308 record.

Back home in England Cook failed to reproduce his legacy of Lord's centuries. Scoring 61 in the only England innings of the first Test which was his only score over fifty from the four innings in England's successful series.His poor form in the long format led to him being omitted for the Twenty20 series and all but the final one-day match.

- *Alastair Cook bowled his first Test over against South Africa at Lord's.*

With a year to go before the 2009 Ashes, it was imperative for Cook to cement his position as opener in the home series against South Africa. Again, at Lord's, Cook made his way comfortably to a half-century before being dismissed for 60. A high team score, together with a benevolent wicket, saw the fifth day bring Cook's first Test over as a bowler: he conceded just one run. Cook fell in one innings of each Test between fifty and a hundred, amassing the considerable average of 47 for the series.

Once again Cook found himself omitted from the Twenty20 and one-day team both for the home series against South Africa as well as the majority of the away series in India, where a string of poor England performances saw him called up for the fifth and ultimately the final match after the terrorist attacks in Mumbai.When the Tests arrived, Cook continued to notch a half-century in one innings of each match, but was outshone by opening partner Strauss's centuries.

- *Alastair Cook 2009: West Indies and Australia*

After India, England toured the West Indies under the new captaincy of Andrew Strauss after Pietersen's brief tenure ended in controversy. Cook was shown still to have the selectors' confidence despite his lack of centuries when he was given the unofficial vice-captaincy before the tour began. The title gave him a boost: he went on to score two fifties in the first warm-up match, retiring out in the second innings but contrasted that with a duck in the next tour match.Similarly, in the First Test he scored four and another duck. After the third Test was abandoned due to the poor quality of the surface, Cook was again beleaguered by his perennial problem: he scored two half centuries against opening partner Strauss's 169.

He seemed to have put it behind him in the first innings of the next Test, however, as he and Strauss put on a record opening stand of 229. Strauss was bowled first for 169 as Cook reached the nineties but fell shortly thereafter for 94. After two days' batting on a benign pitch, the West Indies declared on 749 for nine in response to England's 600 for six. Put back in with one day to spare, Strauss fell for 33, but, after 38 innings' and fifteen months' waiting, Cook finally arrived at his eighth Test century, and went on to pass his highest score with an unbeaten 139 before play ended in a draw. During this innings, Cook also became the youngest Englishman to pass 3,000 Test runs.

England returned home, only to face the West Indies once more. The Second Test took the sides to the Riverside in Durham where, on a benign surface, Cook battled through the first day. After Strauss fell in the morning session, Cook began a partnership with Ravi Bopara, who had recently been promoted to third in the batting order. Over the first day, the two navigated a slow partnership, both strike rates remaining under 55, but, once Cook reached his ninth Test century, Bopara matched it with his own, culminating in a 213-run partnership at Bopara's fall in the closing overs of the day; Cook ended unbeaten on 126. After the second day of play was completely washed out, Cook recorded his first Test 150 and subsequently his then-highest score of 160.

Omitted from the World Twenty20 competition, Cook returned to Essex for two moderate county matches but impressive Twenty20 games. Despite being the only Englishman to score a century, or even more than 50, in the first innings of England's warm up match against Warwickshire, in the first Ashes Test at Cardiff, Cook was the lowest scoring recognised batsman, scoring 10 and 6 – caught in the gully in the first innings, and trapped LBW by Mitchell Johnson in the second. Cook bounced back in the second Test at Lord's, batting through to the afternoon session, as he and his captain Andrew Strauss (who scored 161) set the record for the highest opening English partnership at Lord's with 196, Cook initially scored faster than Strauss but fell short of another Lord's century, trapped again by Johnson for 95.

This partnership, along with Strauss' anchoring throughout the innings, led England to a total of 425 and enabled them to gain a 210-run first-innings lead, aided by three catches from Cook off James Anderson and Stuart Broad. Batting quickly in the second innings to force victory, Cook scored 32 from 54 balls before again falling LBW but providing enough for England to cement their first victory over Australia at Lord's since 1934 and second since 1896.

- *Alastair Cook 2011: World Cup, Sri Lanka and India*

Following England's quarter-final departure from the 2011 World Cup, Andrew Strauss resigned the ODI captaincy and Cook was named his successor, despite not having featured in an ODI since leading the side in Bangladesh. In addition to Cook's promotion, seam bowler Stuart Broad was named captain of the Twenty20 side and England went into the home series with Sri Lanka with different captains for each format of the game.

In the Test series against Sri Lanka Cook made 133 in the first Test of the series to help England take a 1–0 lead. His good form continues into the next match where he made scores of 96 and 106. In the final match of the series Cook made 55 in his only innings of the match, meaning he had scored two centuries and two half centuries in his four innings. Cook's first game as full-time captain against Sri Lanka at the Oval saw England victorious by 110 runs. England went on to win the series 3–2, with Cook top scoring for England in the series with 298 runs in five matches. This performance also led to an ODI player of the series award.

Cook was expected to be a key player when England met India, with the series winners taking over the world number one spot. Although Cook failed to make a significant score in the first game, England won the match to go 1–0 up. Cook only scored seven runs in the entire match in the next game, although England again won to go 2–0 up. In the third match of the series Cook hit a brilliant 294 to help England win the game by an innings and clinch the World's number one spot. In the final match of the series he made 34 as England won the series 4–0. In the second ODI Cook made an unbeaten 80 to help guide England to victory. After making scores of 23 and 12 in the next two matches, Cook finished off the series in good form, making 50 in the final game as England won by six wickets.

For his performances in 2011, he was named in the World Test XI by the ICC and Cricinfo.

England then travelled to India for a limited overs series overseas. Cook scored 60 in the first match but England lost by 126 runs. He scored just 13 runs in the next three games, which included being dismissed for a duck. In the final match of the series he returned to form, making 60. However, England again lost and suffered a 5–0 series defeat.

- *Alastair Cook 2012: Pakistan, Sri Lanka and West Indies*

In the winter of 2012, England struggled in Test matches in the sub continent. They were beaten by Pakistan in the first match of the series, with Cook being dismissed for single figures in both innings. He made 94 in the next game, the only time he passed 50 in the tour, but it was not enough to prevent England losing the match and going 2–0 down. Cook was out cheaply in the first innings as England were again bowled out for less than 200, and although he made 49 in the next innings it wasn't enough to prevent another England defeat.

In the first Test against Sri Lanka England's form showed no sign of improving and they lost the first match of the series, with Cook being dismissed for a duck in the first innings. With the pressure on England going into the final match of the two Test series, Cook returned to his best, making 94 in the first innings before hitting an unbeaten 49 to help England level the series at 1–1.

Back at home against the West Indies, Cook continued to perform well, hitting a half century in the first match of the series. England went on to win the match by five wickets. They also won the next match of the series, with Cook performing well and making an unbeaten 43 in England's second innings to help guide them to victory. The final match of the series ended in a draw. After being dismissed for a duck in the first ODI, Cook made a superb 112 in the second to help England win the match by 8 wickets.

- *Alastair Cook 2012–13: South Africa and India*

England struggled in the three match series against South Africa, eventually losing the series 2–0. Cook started the series well, making yet another century in the first innings of the first match between the two sides. However, he was dismissed for a duck in the second innings as South

Africa took a 1–0 lead. The next match ended in a draw, with Cook making decent contributions, despite failing to pass fifty. The third match was over shadowed when Kevin Pietersen was dropped following an argument with senior England players. Cook scored just ten runs in the match as England lost to lose the series 2–0 and lose their spot at the top of the Test rankings. Cook had an unsuccessful ODI series, the only 50 he made coming in the final match of the series. England lost the match and series finished 2–2.

Cook batting during the third Test during the 2013 Ashes in England. England won the series 3–0; it was Cook's first Ashes series as captain.

- *Alastair Cook 2013: New Zealand and Champions Trophy*

After the tour of India, Cook led England in New Zealand. In the second ODI, Cook hit 78 to guide England to victory and level the series 1–1. England clinched the series by winning the decider, in which Cook made 46 to secure the series for England. In the first Test match, Cook made a century to help England battle to a draw after a poor showing in the first innings. Cook was not at his best in the final two games of the two, although the nature of the wickets meant that the batsmen found it easy to score runs, and so the series ended 0–0. Despite the pitches, many had expected England to win the series and the draw was seen as a disappointment.

Cook led England in the 2013 Champions trophy, and they won their first game against Australia. It was also Cook's first game as captain against Australia. Cook made 59 against Sri Lanka, but England lost the game meaning they were not assured of their place in the next round. Cook top scored with 64 as England narrowly beat New Zealand to book their place in the semi final. After beating South Africa in the semi finals, England played India in the final in what turned out to be a rain affected match. Despite restricting India to 129 in 20 overs, England lost the match by 5 runs, leaving them as runners up. Cook was named as part of the 'Team of the Tournament' by Cricinfo.

In the first Test against New Zealand on home soil, Cook got made good starts in both innings but was unable to convert these scores past fifty. Despite this England won the Test match. In the second match, Cook returned to form, making 130 and leading England to a 2–0 series win. This meant that England remained undefeated in Test series under Cook, winning two and drawing one. Cook played in the ODI series, despite calls for him to be rested ahead of the Ashes. He made scores of 30, 34 and 0 in the three match series, with England losing 2–1.

- *Alastair Cook 2016: Pakistan*

Cook broke India great Sunil Gavaskar's record of 9,607 for the most runs as a Test opener while making 81 against Pakistan in the first Test at Lord's. However, Cook could only make eight in the second innings and England lost the opening Test by 75 runs. On 22 July 2016, Alastair Cook equalled Don Bradman's record of having hit 29 Test centuries when he scored 105 on the opening day of the 2nd Test against Pakistan at Old Trafford. He chose not to enforce the follow-on when England were far ahead in the second Test – but was vindicated by an England victory, with Cook scoring an unbeaten 76 in England's second innings. In the third Test he made scores of 45 and 66 and England won by 141 runs to go 2–1 up in the series. However, England lost the final match, with Cook scoring 35 in the first innings before making seven in the second innings as England lost by 10 wickets and the series ended in a 2–2 tie.

- *Alastair Cook 2016: Bangladesh*

In the first Test against Bangladesh, Cook scored 4 in the first innings and then made 12 in the second. Despite his low scores, England won by 21 runs. In the second Test Cook made 14 in the first innings, and although he made 59 in the second, England were bowled out for 164 to lose the match by 108 runs and draw the series 1–1.

- *Alastair Cook 2018: Pakistan, India and international retirement*

After a score of 70 of the first match of the home series against Pakistan, Cook had another slump in form, scoring a total of 155 more runs in 5 further matches Pakistan and India.On 3 September 2018, after the conclusion of the fourth Test, Cook announced that his twelve-year international career would end at the conclusion of the series against India.On the fourth day of the fifth Test (after resuming on an overnight score of 46*), Cook made a score of 147 and in doing so became the fifth batsman to score a century in his first and last Test match and the second batsman to score twin fifties in his first and last Test. When he reached 76 during the innings, he overtook Kumar Sangakkara to become the fifth-highest run-scorer and the highest-scoring left-hander in Test history.

- *Outside cricket*

Cook has written a column in The Daily Telegraph and Metro. He used his skill with the saxophone to contribute to Freefonix, a CBBC animated series with music-based adventures. Cook has donated his time to various charities including taking part in The Great City Race for Breakthrough Breast Cancer and modelled naked alongside fellow cricketers James Anderson and Stuart Broad to help raise awareness for testicular cancer on behalf of the Everyman Campaign. He is also an active patron of the David Randall Foundation, a charity that carries the name of his childhood friend and opening partner at Maldon CC & Essex age group sides. Much of the proceeds from his 2014 Benefit Year went to this charity.

In December 2011, Cook married Alice Hunt, whom he had known since childhood. The couple have two daughters and one son. He was allowed to miss two tour games in Bangladesh to be present at the birth of the second child in October 2016.

Cook helps maintain a farm near inner urban Leighton Buzzard, and has described farming and cricket as the two passions in his life, stating that "They are both my passions and not many people can say what they do for their job or their life is what they love doing all the time". Cook is a fan of hunting and deer stalking.

CHAPTER TWO

England Cricket Team

- England Cricket Team

1. Disclaimer : During Writing This Book No character & No religious , No Relation Members Are Harmed. It's Only For Study & Entertainment Purpose. Do Not Take Seriously. Short Biopic Written In This Book Written By Mr Vivek Kumar Pandey.

The England cricket team represents England and Wales in international cricket. Since 1997, it has been governed by the England and Wales Cricket Board (ECB), having been previously governed by Marylebone Cricket Club (the MCC) since 1903. England, as a founding nation, is a Full Member of the International Cricket Council (ICC) with Test, One Day International (ODI) and Twenty20 International (T20I) status. Until the 1990s, Scottish and Irish players also played for England as those countries were not yet ICC members in their own right.

England and Australia were the first teams to play a Test match (15–19 March 1877), and along with South Africa, these nations formed the Imperial Cricket Conference (the predecessor to today's International Cricket Council) on 15 June 1909. England and Australia also played the first ODI on 5 January 1971. England's first T20I was played on 13 June 2005, once more against Australia.

As of December 2021, England have played 1,044 Test matches, winning 378 and losing 314 (with 352 draws). In Test series against Australia, England play for The Ashes, one of the most famous trophies in all of sport, and they have won the urn on 32 occasions. England have also played 760 ODIs, winning 383. They have appeared in the final of the Cricket World Cup four times, winning once in 2019; they have also finished as runners-up in two ICC Champions Trophies (2004 and 2013). England have played 143 T20Is, winning 75.They won the ICC T20 World Cup in 2010, and were runners-up in 2016.As of 12 November 2021, England are ranked fourth in Tests, second in ODIs and first in T20Is by the ICC.

- The All-England Eleven in 1846

The first recorded incidence of a team with a claim to represent England comes from 9 July 1739 when an "All-England" team, which consisted of 11 gentlemen from any part of England exclusive of Kent, played against "the Unconquerable County" of Kent and lost by a margin of "very few notches". Such matches were repeated on numerous occasions for the best part of a century.

In 1846 William Clarke formed the All-England Eleven. This team eventually competed against a United All-England Eleven with annual matches occurring between 1847 and 1856. These matches were arguably the most important contest of the English season if judged by the quality of the players.

- Early tours

The first overseas tour occurred in September 1859 with England touring North America. This team had six players from the All-England Eleven, six from the United All-England Eleven and was captained by George Parr.

With the outbreak of the American Civil War, attention turned elsewhere. English tourists visited Australia in 1861–62 with this first tour organised as a commercial venture by Messrs Spiers and Pond, restaurateurs of Melbourne. Most matches played during tours prior to 1877 were "against odds", with the opposing team fielding more than 11 players to make for a more even contest. This first Australian tour were mostly against odds of at least 18/11.

- The first England team to tour southern Australia in 1861–62

The tour was so successful that Parr led a second tour in 1863–64. James Lillywhite led a subsequent England team which sailed on the P&O steamship Poonah on 21 September 1876. They played a combined

Australian XI, for once on even terms of 11-a-side. The match, starting on 15 March 1877 at the Melbourne Cricket Ground came to be regarded as the inaugural Test match. The combined Australian XI won this Test match by 45 runs with Charles Bannerman of Australia scoring the first Test century. At the time, the match was promoted as James Lillywhite's XI v Combined Victoria and New South Wales. The teams played a return match on the same ground at Easter, 1877, when Lillywhite's team avenged their loss with a victory by four wickets. The first Test match on English soil occurred in 1880 with England victorious; this was the first time England fielded a fully representative side with W. G. Grace included in the team.

- 1880s

As a result of this loss, the tour of 1882–83 was dubbed by England captain Ivo Bligh as "the quest to regain the ashes". England, with a mixture of amateurs and professionals, won the series 2–1. Bligh was presented with an urn that contained some ashes, which have variously been said to be of a bail, ball or even a woman's veil, and so The Ashes was born. A fourth match was then played which Australia won by four wickets. However, the match was not considered part of the Ashes series. England dominated many of these early contests with England winning the Ashes series 10 times between 1884 and 1898. During this period England also played their first Test match against South Africa in 1889 at Port Elizabeth.

- 1890s

England won the 1890 Ashes series 2–0, with the third match of the series being the first Test match to be abandoned. England lost 2–1 in the 1891–92 series, although England regained the urn the following year. England again won the 1894–95 series, winning 3–2 under the leadership of Andrew Stoddart. In 1895–96, England played South Africa, winning all Tests in the series. The 1899 Ashes series was the first tour where the MCC and the counties appointed a selection committee. There were three active players: Grace, Lord Hawke and Warwickshire captain Herbert Bainbridge. Prior to this, England teams for home Tests had been chosen by the club on whose ground the match was to be played. England lost the 1899 Ashes series 1–0, with Grace making his final Test appearance in the first match of the series.

• 1900s

The start of the 20th century saw mixed results for England as they lost four of the eight Ashes series between 1900 and 1914. During this period, England lost their first series against South Africa in the 1905–06 season 4–1 as their batting faltered.

England lost their first series of the new century to Australia in 1901–02 Ashes. Australia also won the 1902 series, which was memorable for exciting cricket, including Gilbert Jessop scoring a Test century in just 70 minutes. England regained the Ashes in 1904 under the captaincy of Pelham Warner. R. E. Foster scored 287 on his debut and Wilfred Rhodes took 15 wickets in a match. In 1905–06, England lost 4–1 against South Africa. England avenged the defeat in 1907, when they won the series 1–0 under the captaincy of Foster. However, they lost the 1909 Ashes series against Australia, suing 25 players in the process. England also lost to South Africa, with Jack Hobbs scoring his first of 15 centuries on the tour.

• 1910s

England toured Australia in 1911–12 and beat their opponents 4–1. The team included the likes of Rhodes, Hobbs, Frank Woolley and Sydney Barnes. England lost the first match of the series but bounced back and won the next four Tests. This proved to be the last Ashes series before the war.

The 1912 season saw England take part in a unique experiment. A nine-Test triangular tournament involving England, South Africa and Australia was set up. The series was hampered by a very wet summer and player disputes however and the tournament was considered a failure with the Daily Telegraph stating:

Nine Tests provide a surfeit of cricket, and contests between Australia and South Africa are not a great attraction to the British public.With Australia sending a weakened team and the South African bowlers being ineffective England dominated the tournament winning four of their six matches. The match between Australia and South Africa at Lord's was visited by King George V, the first time a reigning monarch had watched Test cricket. England went on one more tour before the outbreak of the First World War, beating South Africa 4–0, with Barnes taking 49 wickets in the series.

- 1920s

England's first match after the war was in the 1920–21 season against Australia. Still feeling the effects of the war England went down to a series of crushing defeats and suffered their first whitewash losing the series 5–0. Six Australians scored hundreds while Mailey spun out 36 English batsmen. Things were no better in the next few Ashes series losing the 1921 Ashes series 3–0 and the 1924–25 Ashes 4–1. England's fortunes were to change in 1926 as they regained the Ashes and were a formidable team during this period dispatching Australia 4–1 in the 1928–29 Ashes tour.

On the same year the West Indies became the fourth nation to be granted Test status and played their first game against England. England won each of these three Tests by an innings, and a view was expressed in the press that their elevation had proved a mistake although Learie Constantine did the double on the tour. In the 1929–30 season England went on two concurrent tours with one team going to New Zealand (who were granted Test status earlier that year) and the other to the West Indies. Despite sending two separate teams England won both tours beating New Zealand 1–0 and the West Indies 2–1.

- 1930s

The 1930 Ashes series saw a young Don Bradman dominate the tour, scoring 974 runs in his seven Test innings. He scored 254 at Lord's, 334 at Headingley and 232 at The Oval. Australia regained the Ashes winning the series 3–1. As a result of Bradman's prolific run-scoring the England captain Douglas Jardine chose to develop the already existing leg theory into fast leg theory, or bodyline, as a tactic to stop Bradman. Fast leg theory involved bowling fast balls directly at the batsman's body. The batsman would need to defend himself, and if he touched the ball with the bat, he risked being caught by one of a large number of fielders placed on the leg side.

English cricket team at the Test match held at the Brisbane Exhibition Ground. England won the match by a record margin of 675 runs.Using Jardine's fast leg theory, England won the next Ashes series 4–1, but complaints about the Bodyline tactic caused crowd disruption on the tour, and threats of diplomatic action from the Australian Cricket Board, which during the tour sent the following cable to the MCC in London:

Bodyline bowling assumed such proportions as to menace best interests of game, making protection of body by batsmen the main consideration. Causing intensely bitter feeling between players as well as injury. In our opinion is unsportsmanlike. Unless stopped at once likely to upset friendly relations existing between Australia and England.

Later, Jardine was removed from the captaincy and the Laws of Cricket changed so that no more than one fast ball aimed at the body was permitted per over, and having more than two fielders behind square leg was banned.

England's following tour of India in the 1933–34 season was the first Test match to be staged in the subcontinent. The series was also notable for Stan Nichols and Nobby Clark bowling so many bouncers that the Indian batsman wore solar toupées instead of caps to protect themselves.

Australia won the 1934 Ashes series 2–1 and kept the urn for the following 19 years. Many of the wickets of the time were friendly to batsmen resulting in a large proportion of matches ending in high scoring draws and many batting records being set.

England drew the 1938 Ashes, meaning Australia retained the urn. England went into the final match of the series at The Oval 1–0 down, but won the final game by an innings and 579 runs. Len Hutton made the highest ever Test score by an Englishman, making 364 in England first innings to help them reach 903, their highest ever score against Australia.

The 1938–39 tour of South Africa saw another experiment with the deciding Test being a timeless Test that was played to a finish. England lead 1–0 going into the final timeless match at Durban. Despite the final Test being 'timeless‘, the game ended in a draw after 10 days as England had to catch the train to catch the boat home. A record 1,981 runs were scored, and the concept of timeless Tests was abandoned. England went on one final tour of the West Indies in 1939 before the Second World War, although a team for an MCC tour of India was selected more in hope than expectation of the matches being played.

- 1940s

Test cricket resumed after the war in 1946, and England won their first match back against India. However, they struggled in the 1946–47 Ashes series, losing 3–0 in Australia under Wally Hammond's captaincy. England beat South Africa 3–0 in 1947 with Denis Compton scoring 1,187 runs in the series.

The 1947–48 series against the West Indies was another disappointment for England, with the side losing 2–0 following injuries to several key players. England suffered further humiliation against Bradman's invincible side in the 1948 Ashes series. Hutton was controversially dropped for the third Test, and England were bowled out for just 52 at The Oval. The series proved to be Bradman's final Ashes series.

In 1948–49, England beat South Africa 2–0 under the captaincy of George Mann. The series included a record breaking stand of 359 between Hutton and Cyril Washbrook. The decade ended with England drawing the Test series against New Zealand, with every match ending in a draw.

- 1950s

Their fortunes changed on the 1953 Ashes tour as they won the series 1–0. England did not lose a series between their 1950–51 and 1958–59 tours of Australia and secured famous victory in 1954–55 under the captaincy of Len Hutton, thanks to Frank Tyson whose 6/85 at Sydney and 7/27 at Melbourne are remembered as the fastest bowling ever seen in Australia. The 1956 series was remembered for the bowling of Jim Laker who took 46 wickets at an average of 9.62, including figures of 19/90 at Old Trafford. After drawing to South Africa, England defeated the West Indies and New Zealand comfortably.

The England team then left for Australia in the 1958–59 season with a team that had been hailed as the strongest ever to leave on an Ashes tour but lost the series 4–0 as Richie Benaud's revitalised Australians were too strong, with England struggling with the bat throughout the series.

On 24 August 1959, England inflicted its only 5–0 whitewash over India. All out for 194 at The Oval, India lost the last test by an innings. England's batsman Ken Barrington and Colin Cowdrey both had an excellent series with the bat, with Barrington scoring 357 runs across the series and Cowdrey scoring 344.

- 1960s

The early and middle 1960s were poor periods for English cricket. Despite England's strength on paper, Australia held the Ashes and the West Indies dominated England in the early part of the decade. May stood down as captain in 1961 following the 1961 Ashes defeat.

Ted Dexter succeeded him as captain but England continued to suffer indifferent results. In 1961–62, they beat Pakistan, but also lost to India. The following year saw England and Australia tie the 1962–63 Ashes series 1–1, meaning Australia retained the urn. Despite beating New Zealand 3–0, England went on to lose to the West Indies, and again failed in the 1964 Ashes, losing the home series 1–0, which marked the end of Dexter's captaincy.

However, from 1968 to 1971 they played 27 consecutive Test matches without defeat, winning 9 and drawing 18 (including the abandoned Test at Melbourne in 1970–71). The sequence began when they drew with Australia at Lord's in the Second Test of the 1968 Ashes series and ended in 1971 when India won the Third Test at The Oval by four wickets. They played 13 Tests with only one defeat immediately beforehand and so played a total of 40 consecutive Tests with only one defeat, dating from their innings victory over the West Indies at The Oval in 1966. During this period they beat New Zealand, India, the West Indies, and Pakistan, and under Ray Illingworth's leadership, regained The Ashes from Australia in 1970–71.

- 1970s

The 1970s, for the England team, can be largely split into three parts. Early in the decade, Illingworth's side dominated world cricket, winning the Ashes away in 1971 and then retaining them at home in 1972. The same side beat Pakistan at home in 1971 and played by far the better cricket against India that season. However, England were largely helped by the rain to sneak the Pakistan series 1–0 but the same rain saved India twice and one England collapse saw them lose to India. This was, however, one of (if not the) strongest England team ever with the likes of Illingworth, Geoffrey Boycott, John Edrich, Basil D'Oliveira, Dennis Amiss, Alan Knott, John Snow and Derek Underwood at its core.

The mid-1970s were more turbulent. Illingworth and several others had refused to tour India in 1972–73 which led to a clamour for Illingworth's job by the end of that summer – England had just been beaten 2–0 by a flamboyant West Indies side – with several England players well over 35. Mike Denness was the surprising choice but only lasted 18 months; his results against poor opposition were good, but England were badly exposed as ageing and lacking in good fast bowling against the 1974–75 Australians, losing that series 4–1 to lose the Ashes.

Denness was replaced in 1975 by Tony Greig. While he managed to avoid losing to Australia, his side were largely thrashed the following year by the young and very much upcoming West Indies for whom Greig's infamous "grovel" remark acted as motivation. Greig's finest hour was probably the 1976–77 win over India in India. When Greig was discovered as being instrumental in World Series Cricket, he was sacked, and replaced by Mike Brearley.

Brearley's side showed again the hyperbole that is often spoken when one side dominates in cricket. While his side of 1977–80 contained some young players who went on to become England greats, most notably future captains Ian Botham, David Gower and Graham Gooch, their opponents were often very much weakened by the absence of their World Series players, especially in 1978, when England beat New Zealand 3–0 and Pakistan 2–0 before thrashing what was effectively Australia's 2nd XI 5–1 in 1978–79.

- 1980s

The England team, with Brearley's exit in 1980, was never truly settled throughout the 1980s, which will probably be remembered as a low point for the team. While some of the great players like Botham, Gooch and Gower had fine careers, the team seldom succeeded in beating good opposition throughout the decade and did not score a home Test victory between September 1985 and July 1990.

Botham took over the captaincy in 1980 and they put up a good fight against the West Indies, losing a five match Test series 1–0, although England were humbled in the return series. After scoring a pair in the first Test against Australia, Botham lost the captaincy due to his poor form, and was replaced by Brearley. Botham returned to form and played exceptionally in the remainder of the series, being named man of the match in the third, fourth and fifth Tests. The series became known as Botham's Ashes as England recorded a 3–1 victory.

Keith Fletcher took over as captain in 1981, but England lost his first series in charge against India. Bob Willis took over as captain in 1982 and enjoyed victories over India and Pakistan, but lost the Ashes after Australia clinched the series 2–1. England hosted the World Cup in 1983 and reached the semi-finals, but their Test form remained poor, as they suffered defeats against New Zealand, Pakistan and the West Indies.

Gower took over as skipper in 1984 and led the team to a 2–1 victory over India. They went on to win the 1985 Ashes 3–1, although after this came a poor run of form. Defeat to the West Indies dented the team's confidence, and they went on to lose to India 2–0. In 1986, Micky Stewart was appointed the first full-time England coach. England beat New Zealand, but there was little hope of them retaining the Ashes in 1986–87. However, despite being described as a team that 'can't bat, can't bowl and can't field', they went on to win the series 2–1.

After losing consecutive series against Pakistan, England drew a three match Test series against New Zealand 0–0. They reached the final of the 1987 World Cup, but lost by seven runs against Australia. After losing 4–0 to the West Indies, England lost the Ashes to a resurgent Australia led by Allan Border. With the likes of Gooch banned following a rebel tour to South Africa, a new look England side suffered defeat again against the West Indies, although this time by a margin of 2–1.

- 1990s

If the 1980s were a low point for English Test cricket, then the 1990s were only a slight improvement. The arrival of Gooch as captain in 1990 forced a move toward more professionalism and especially fitness though it took some time for old habits to die. Even in 2011, one or two successful county players have been shown up as physically unfit for international cricket. Creditable performances against India and New Zealand in 1990 were followed by a hard-fought draw against the 1991 West Indies and a strong performance in the 1992 Cricket World Cup in which the England team finished as runners-up for the second consecutive World Cup, but landmark losses against Australia in 1990–91 and especially Pakistan in 1992 showed England up badly in terms of bowling. So bad was England's bowling in 1993 that Rod Marsh described England's pace attack at one point as "pie throwers". Having lost three of the first four Tests played in England in 1993, Gooch resigned to be replaced by Michael Atherton.

More selectorial problems abounded during Atherton's reign as new chairman of selectors and coach Ray Illingworth (then into his 60s) assumed almost sole responsibility for the team off the field. The youth policy which had seen England emerge from the West Indies tour of 1993–94 with some credit (though losing to a seasoned Windies team) was abandoned and players such as Gatting and Gooch were persisted with when well into their 30s and 40s. England continued to do well at home against weaker opponents such as India, New Zealand and a West Indies side beginning to fade but struggled badly against improving sides like Pakistan and South Africa.

Atherton had offered his resignation after losing the 1997 Ashes series 3–2 having been 1–0 up after two matches – eventually to resign one series later in early 1998. England, looking for talent, went through a whole raft of new players during this period, such as Ronnie Irani, Adam Hollioake, Craig White, Graeme Hick and Mark Ramprakash. At this time, there were two main problems:The lack of a genuine all-rounder to bat at 6, Botham having left a huge gap in the batting order when he retired from Tests in 1992.

Alec Stewart, a sound wicket-keeper and an excellent player of quick bowling, could not open and keep wicket, hence his batting down the order, where he was often exposed to spin which he did not play as well.

Stewart took the reins as captain in 1998, but another losing Ashes series and early World Cup exit cost him Test and ODI captaincy in 1999. This should not detract from the 1998 home Test series where England showed great fortitude to beat a powerful South African side 2–1.

Another reason for their poor performances were the demands of County Cricket teams on their players, meaning that England could rarely field a full-strength team on their tours. This eventually led to the ECB taking over from the MCC as the governing body of England and the implementation of central contracts. 1992 also saw Scotland sever ties with the England and Wales team, and begin to compete as the Scotland national team.

By 1999, with coach David Lloyd resigning after the World Cup exit and new captain Nasser Hussain just appointed, England hit rock bottom after losing 2–1 to New Zealand in shambolic fashion. Hussain was booed on the Oval balcony as the crowd jeered "We've got the worst team in the world" to the tune of "He's Got the Whole World in His Hands".

- 2000s

Central contracts were installed – reducing players workloads – and following the arrival of Zimbabwean coach Duncan Fletcher, England thrashed the fallen West Indies 3–1. England's results in Asia improved that winter with series wins against both Pakistan and Sri Lanka. Hussain's side had a far harder edge to it, avoiding the anticipated "Greenwash" in the 2001

Ashes series against the all-powerful Australian team. The nucleus the side was slowly coming together as players such as Hussain himself, Graham Thorpe, Darren Gough and Ashley Giles began to be regularly selected. By 2003 though, having endured another Ashes drubbing as well as another first-round exit from the World Cup, Hussain resigned as captain after one Test against South Africa.

Michael Vaughan took over, with players encouraged to express themselves. England won five consecutive Test series prior to facing Australia in the 2005 Ashes series, taking the team to second place in the ICC Test Championship table. During this period England defeated the West Indies home and away, New Zealand, and Bangladesh at home, and South Africa in South Africa. In June 2005, England played its first ever T20 international match, defeating Australia by 100 runs. Later that year, England defeated Australia 2–1 in a thrilling series to regain the Ashes for the first time in 16 years, having lost them in 1989. Following the 2005 Ashes win, the team suffered from a spate of serious injuries to key players such as Vaughan, Giles, Andrew Flintoff and Simon Jones. As a result, the team underwent an enforced period of transition. A 2–0 defeat in Pakistan was followed by two drawn away series with India and Sri Lanka.

In the home Test series victory against Pakistan in July and August 2006, several promising new players emerged. Most notable were the left-arm orthodox spin bowler Monty Panesar, the first Sikh to play Test cricket for England, and left-handed opening batsman Alastair Cook. The 2006–07 Ashes series was keenly anticipated and was expected to provide a level of competition comparable to the 2005 series. In the event, England, captained by Flintoff who was deputising for the injured Vaughan, lost all five Tests to concede the first Ashes whitewash in 86 years.

In the 2007 Cricket World Cup, England lost to most of the Test playing nations they faced, beating only the West Indies and Bangladesh, although they also avoided defeat by any of the non-Test playing nations. Even so, the unimpressive nature of most of their victories in the tournament, combined with heavy defeats by New Zealand, Australia and South Africa, left many commentators criticising the manner in which the England team approached the one-day game. Coach Duncan Fletcher resigned after eight years in the job as a result and was succeeded by former Sussex coach Peter Moores.

In 2007–08, England toured Sri Lanka and New Zealand, losing the first series 1–0 and winning the second 2–1. These series were followed up at home in May 2008 with a 2–0 home series win against New Zealand, with the results easing pressure on Moores – who was not at ease with his team, particularly star batsman Kevin Pietersen. Pietersen succeeded Vaughan as captain in June 2008, after England had been well beaten by South Africa at home. The poor relationship between the two came to a head on the 2008–09 tour to India. England lost the series 1–0 and both men resigned their positions, although Pietersen remained a member of the England team. Moores was replaced as coach by Zimbabwean Andy Flower. Against this background, England toured the West Indies under the captaincy of Andrew Strauss and, in a disappointing performance, lost the Test series 1–0.

The 2009 Ashes series featured the first Test match played in Wales, at Sophia Gardens, Cardiff. England drew the match thanks to a last-wicket stand by bowlers James Anderson and Panesar. A victory for each team followed before the series was decided at The Oval. Thanks to fine bowling by Stuart Broad and Graeme Swann and a debut century by Jonathan Trott, England regained the Ashes.

- 2010s

After a drawn Test series in South Africa, England won their first ever ICC world championship, the 2010 World Twenty20, with a seven-wicket win over Australia in Barbados. The following winter in the 2010–11 Ashes, they beat Australia 3–1 to retain the urn and record their first series win in Australia for 24 years. Furthermore, all three of their wins were by an innings – the first time a touring side had ever recorded three innings victories in a single Test series. Cook earned Man of the Series with 766 runs.

England struggled to match their Test form in the 2011 Cricket World Cup. Despite beating South Africa and tying with eventual winners India, England suffered shock losses to Ireland and Bangladesh before losing in the quarter-finals to Sri Lanka.However the team's excellent form in the Test match arena continued and on 13 August 2011, they became the world's top-ranked Test team after comfortably whitewashing India 4–0, their sixth consecutive series victory and eighth in the past nine series. However, this status only lasted a year – having lost 3–0 to Pakistan over the winter, England were beaten 2–0 by South Africa, who replaced them at the top of the rankings. It was their first home series loss since 2008, against the same opposition.

This loss saw the resignation of Strauss as captain (and his retirement from cricket). Cook, who was already in charge of the ODI side, replaced Strauss and led England to a 2–1 victory in India – their first in the country since 1984–85. In doing so, he became the first captain to score centuries in his first five Tests as captain and became England's leading century-maker with 23 centuries to his name.

- The England team celebrate victory over Australia in the 2015 Ashes series

After finishing as runners-up in the ICC Champions Trophy, England faced Australia in back-to-back Ashes series. A 3–0 home win secured England the urn for the fourth time in five series. However, in the return series, they found themselves utterly demolished in a 5–0 defeat, their second Ashes whitewash in under a decade. Their misery was compounded by batsman Jonathan Trott leaving the tour early due to a stress-related illness and the mid-series retirement of spinner Graeme Swann. Following the tour, head coach Flower resigned his post while Pietersen was dropped indefinitely from the England team.

Flower was replaced by his predecessor, Moores, but he was sacked for a second time after a string of disappointing results including failing to advance from the group stage at the 2015 World Cup. He was replaced by Australian Trevor Bayliss who oversaw an upturn of form in the ODI side, including series victories against New Zealand and Pakistan. In the Test arena, England reclaimed the Ashes 3–2 in the summer of 2015.

England entered the 2019 Cricket World Cup as favourites, having been ranked the number one ODI side by the ICC for over a year prior to the tournament. However, shock defeats to Pakistan and Sri Lanka during the group stage left them on the brink of elimination and needing to win their final two games against India and New Zealand to guarantee progression to the semi-finals. This was achieved, putting their campaign back on track, and an eight-wicket victory over Australia in the semi-final at Edgbaston meant England were in their first World Cup final since 1992. The final against New Zealand at Lord's has been described as one of the greatest and most dramatic matches in the history of cricket, with some calling it the "greatest ODI in history", as both the match and subsequent Super Over were tied, after England went into the final over of their innings 14 runs behind New Zealand's total. England won by virtue of having scored more boundaries throughout the match, securing their maiden World Cup title in their fourth final appearance.

- England and Wales Cricket Board

The England and Wales Cricket Board (ECB) is the governing body of English cricket and the England cricket team. The Board has been operating since 1 January 1997 and represents England on the International Cricket Council. The ECB is also responsible for the generation of income from the sale of tickets, sponsorship and broadcasting rights, primarily in relation to the England team. The ECB's income in the 2006 calendar year was £77 million.

Prior to 1997, the Test and County Cricket Board (TCCB) was the governing body for the English team. Apart from in Test matches, when touring abroad, the England team officially played as MCC up to and including the 1976–77 tour of Australia, reflecting the time when MCC had been responsible for selecting the touring party. The last time the England touring team wore the bacon-and-egg colours of the MCC was on the 1996–97 tour of New Zealand.

- Status of Wales

Historically, the England team represented the whole of Great Britain in international cricket, with Scottish or Welsh national teams playing sporadically and players from both countries occasionally representing England. Scotland became an independent member of the ICC in 1994, having severed links with the TCCB two years earlier.

Criticism has been made of the England and Wales Cricket Board using only the England name while utilising Welsh players such as Simon and Geraint Jones. With Welsh players pursuing international careers exclusively with an England team, there have been a number of calls for Wales to become an independent member of the ICC, or for the ECB to provide more fixtures for a Welsh national team.However, both Cricket Wales and Glamorgan County Cricket Club have continually supported the ECB, with Glamorgan arguing for the financial benefits of the Welsh county within the English structure, and Cricket Wales stating they are "committed to continuing to play a major role within the ECB".

The absence of a Welsh cricket team has seen a number of debates within the Welsh Senedd. In 2013 a debate saw both Conservative and Labour members lend their support to the establishment of an independent Welsh team.

In 2015, a report produced by the Welsh National Assembly's petitions committee, reflected the passionate debate around the issue. Bethan Jenkins, Plaid Cymru's spokesperson on heritage, culture, sport and broadcasting, and a member of the petitions committee, argued that Wales should have its own international team and withdraw from the ECB. Jenkins noted that Ireland (with a population of 6.4 million) was an ICC member with 6,000 club players whereas Wales (with 3 million) had 7,500. Jenkins said: "Cricket Wales and Glamorgan CCC say the idea of a Welsh national cricket team is 'an emotive subject', of course having a national team is emotive, you only have to look at the stands during any national game to see that. To suggest this as anything other than natural is a bit of a misleading argument."

In 2017, the First Minister of Wales, Carwyn Jones called for the reintroduction of the Welsh one-day team stating: "[It] is odd that we see Ireland and Scotland playing in international tournaments and not Wales."

- England at 2021

In February 2021, England and Wales Cricket Board announced that England's Principal partner NatWest has been replaced by Cinch, an online used car marketplace. England's kit is manufactured by New Balance, who replaced previous manufacturer Adidas in April 2017.

When playing Test cricket, England's cricket whites feature the three lions badge on the left of the shirt and the name of the sponsor Cinch on the centre. English fielders may wear a navy blue cap or white sun hat with the ECB logo in the middle. Helmets are also coloured navy blue. Before 1997 the uniform sported the TCCB lion and stumps logo on the uniforms, while the helmets, jumpers and hats had the three lions emblem.

In limited overs cricket, England's ODI and Twenty20 shirts feature the Cinch logo across the centre, with the three lions badge on the left of the shirt and the New Balance logo on the right. In ODIs, the kit comprises a blue shirt with navy trousers, whilst the Twenty20 kit comprises a flame red shirt and navy trousers. In ICC limited-overs tournaments, a modified kit design is used with sponsor's logo moving to the sleeve and 'ENGLAND' printed across the front.

Over the years, England's ODI kit has cycled between various shades of blue (such as a pale blue used until the mid-1990s, when it was replaced in favour of a bright blue) with the occasional all-red kit.In April 2017, ECB brought back traditional cable-knit sweater for test matches under new supplier New Balance.

CHAPTER THREE

History of the England cricket

- History of the England cricket

The history of the England cricket team can be said to date back to at least 1739, when sides styled "Kent" and "All England" played a match at Bromley Common. Over 300 matches involving "England" or "All England" prior to 1877 are known. However these teams were usually put together on an ad hoc basis and were rarely fully representative.

The history of the current England side can be traced to 1877 when England played in what was subsequently recognised as the very first Test match. Since then, up to 20 August 2006 they have played 852 Test matches, winning 298, losing 245 and drawing 309. During these 852 matches, they have been captained by 77 different players.

- Early history

The term "All-England" was first used in reports of two Kent v All-England matches in July 1739.

The first match was at Bromley Common in Kent on Monday 9 July 1739. It was billed as between "eleven gentlemen of that county (i.e., Kent) and eleven gentlemen from any part of England, exclusive of Kent". Kent, described as "the Unconquerable County" won by "a very few notches".

The second match was at the Artillery Ground in Bunhill Fields, Finsbury on Monday 23 July 1739. This game was drawn and a report includes the phrase "eleven picked out of all England".

In subsequent decades there were many more such matches between a side representing a county, or the MCC, and a side drawn from the rest of England and described as "England" or "All England". As the next section describes, in 1846 the term "All England Eleven" would acquire a new, more precise, definition.

- The All-England XI

In 1846 William Clarke formed the All-England Eleven as a touring team of leading players to play matches at big city venues, mainly in the North of England. Clarke's team was a top-class side worthy of its title. The AEE lasted until 1880. In 1852, several players set up the United All-England Eleven as a rival to the AEE, and from 1857 to 1866 the annual match between these two teams was arguably the most important contest of the English season – certainly judged by the quality of the players.

- The 1873/4 team.

The early overseas tours were organised as purely commercial ventures, as indeed were the first Test-playing tours. The first such tour was to North America by a team of English professionals, departing England in September 1859. The team comprised six players from the All-England Eleven and six from the United All-England Eleven, and was captained by George Parr. They played five matches, winning them all. There were no first-class fixtures.

With the outbreak of the American Civil War, attention turned to Australia. The inaugural tour of the country took place in 1861–2, and was organised by Messrs Spiers & Pond. Led by HH Stephenson, the English team played 12 matches, but none were first-class.

In 1863–4, the Melbourne Cricket Club organised a tour by an English team under the captaincy of George Parr, which also visited New Zealand. The team played 16 matches, but none were first-class.

There were further tours of North America (taking in both the US and Canada) in late 1868, led by Edgar Willsher, and in late 1872, under R.A. Fitzgerald. The latter side included W.G.Grace.

In 1873–4, the Melbourne Cricket Club organised a tour by a team under the captaincy of WG Grace, which played 15 matches, but none were first-class.

Most of the matches of these early touring teams were played "against odds", that is to say the opposing team was permitted to have more than eleven players (usually twenty-two) in order to make a more even contest.

- 1877 to 1890

James Lillywhite, a professional with Sussex CCC, led a team which had sailed on the P&O steamship Poonah on 21 September 1876. They played in Australia and then New Zealand before returning to Australia to play a combined Australian XI, for once on even terms of XI a side. The match, starting on 15 March 1877 at the Melbourne Cricket Ground, came to be regarded as the first Test match, although none of its participants could have guessed at its significance at the time. Charles Bannerman, of Australia, faced the first ball and scored the first century, a glorious 165 before retiring hurt with a broken finger. The next highest score in this inaugural Test for Australia was Tom Horan with 10. Alfred Shaw of England bowled the first ball and took 5 for 38 in Australia's second innings. Tom Kendall, born in England, took 7 English wickets for 55 to bring Australia victory by 45 runs. 100 years later, in the Centenary Test, the result and margin would be exactly the same. England won a second match to square the series.

In 1878/79 Kent captain and MCC luminary Lord Harris took a team, consisting mainly of amateurs, to Australia where they lost by 10 wickets at Melbourne. Their batting was reasonably strong but the lack of professional bowlers cost them dear. The tour became famous for an unseemly incident in a tour game at Sydney where a near riot broke out. One of the umpires was Edmund Barton, who became Australia's first prime minister.

The 1880 Australian tourists were the first to play a Test match on English soil. Their 'demon' bowler, Fred Spofforth, sustained a hand injury and, crucially, missed the game in which W.G. Grace scored 152 and Billy Murdoch one run better. Lord Harris led the victorious England side at the Oval.

An all professional side, organised by Shaw, Shrewsbury and Lillywhite sailed to Australia for the 1881/82 campaign. The tour was bedeviled with scandal and allegations of fisticuffs, betting and heavy drinking. Tom Garrett took 18 wickets in the three Tests played for Australia. Many of the tour matches were still against local '22's. Australia won the four Test series 2 – 0.

The developing rivalry took on a new turn in 1882, when England lost at home at The Oval in the solitary Test of the summer. Spofforth took 7 for 46 and 7 for 44 and Ted Peate, Yorkshire slow left armer who had taken 8 wickets, was out just 8 runs short of victory. Upset at this turn of events, The Sporting Times printed an obituary to English cricket: "In

Affectionate Remembrance of ENGLISH CRICKET, which died at the Oval on 29th AUGUST 1882, Deeply lamented by a large circle of sorrowing friends and acquaintances R.I.P. N.B. – The body will be cremated and the ashes taken to Australia."

When England toured Australia the following winter of 1882/83 and won 2–1, the England captain, the Hon. Ivo Bligh was presented with an urn that contained some ashes, which have variously been said to be of a bail, ball or even a woman's veil. And so The Ashes series was born. Yorkshire stalwart Billy Bates, who played all his 15 Tests on 5 tours to Australia, scored 55 and took 14 for 102 at Melbourne in the second Test, including the first Test hat-trick, to bring England the first innings victory in Test cricket. A.G. Steel made 135* at Sydney – although he did drop Bonner 4 times (out of 8 drops in total) as the giant Australian hitter scored 87.

England won 1–0 in the three Test series in 1884. Peate took 6 for 85 in Australia's first innings, and Ulyett 7 for 36, the second as England won by an innings Lord's where Steel made a wonderful 148 out of England's first innings of 379. Australia's captain Billy Murdoch scored the first Test double hundred at the Oval where Walter Read of England hit a century in 113 minutes after going in at number 10. All 11 Englishmen bowled in Australia's innings, including wicket keeper Lyttelton with underarm lobs.

England embarked on a long stretch of dominance. They won 14 and lost only 3 of the Tests played between 1884 and 1890. Billy Barnes hit 134 in the opening Adelaide Test of the five Test 1884/85 series while Johnny Briggs of Lancashire hit a two-hour ton at Melbourne in the second, where Australia fielded a completely new team of 11 different players after a dispute over gate money. Wilfred Flowers scored 56 and took 5 for 46 in the third Test at Sydney where Australia pulled back a game thanks to Bonner smashing a century in even time. England won the deciding fifth Test by an innings at Melbourne, Arthur Shrewsbury making 105*.

W. G. Grace scored 170 in the Oval Test of 1886, beating the individual Test innings record of 164 set by Arthur Shrewsbury in the previous match on an evil pitch at Lords. England won by an innings on the third day after Australia were bowled out for 68 and 149m with George Lohmann of Surrey taking 12 for 104. The Australian tourists, without Bannerman or Murdoch and often losing Spofforth to injuries, lost all three Tests.

Shrewsbury's England beat Australia in both matches on the 1886–87 tour, despite being bowled out for 45 on the first day at Sydney. Two England parties toured there in 1887–88, with Shaw and Shrewsbury's team sponsored by Melbourne CC and Lord Harris's team by the Sydney Association. The two sides joined up for one Test Match at Sydney which they won thanks to Lohmann's 9 wickets and Bobby Peel's 10. Australia made just 42 and 82 on a poor pitch in bad light.

The 1888 Australians won at Lords but lost at The Oval and Old Trafford. Their bowling was penetrative, particularly Jack Ferris and the 'terror' Charlie Turner, but their batting was too weak to withstand the English professionals in their home conditions. Bobby Peel took 11 wickets at Old Trafford.

England won the first Test in South Africa, at Port Elizabeth in March 1889 by 8 wickets, despite fielding a less than first choice XI. W.H. Ashley took 7 for 95 for South Africa in his only Test. Bobby Abel of Surrey scored 120 for England in the Second Test, the first hundred scored in South Africa. Bernard Tancred of South Africa became the first Test batsman to carry his bat, for 26*, as South Africa collapsed to 47 all out. M.P. Bowden remains the youngest man to captain England, at just 23 years and 144 days. Johnny Briggs took 7 for 17 and 8 for 11 at Cape Town, 14 bowled and 1 LBW.

- 1890s

Four ball overs gave way to five ball overs in the 1890s and to six ball overs in Australia, as the game continued to develop quickly. England won the 1890 Ashes series 2–0, although Jack Barrett carried his bat for 67 through Australia's second innings of 176 at Lord's. W. G. Grace was out second ball in the first innings but saw England home in the second with 75*. Frederick Martin took 12 Australian wickets for 102 but 'Nutty' never played an Ashes match again. The third scheduled match, at Old Trafford, was the first Test to be abandoned without a ball being bowled.

W. G. Grace's tourists lost 2–1 on the 1891–92 tour, Australia winning at Melbourne and Sydney, where Bannerman batted for seven and a half hours and scored only three boundaries and England's Bobby Abel carried his bat for 132. England claimed a consolation innings victory at Adelaide where Stoddard scored 134 and Peel 83 and Briggs took 6 wickets in each innings.

England won the only Test on the 1891/92 tour of South Africa at Cape Town, where Harry Wood, the Surrey wicket keeper made 134 not out and Ferris, who had earlier played for Australia, took 13 for 91. Billy Murdoch was another Australian turned Englishman on the tour.

- England regained the Ashes in 1893, with an innings win at The Oval and draws in the other two Tests. W. G. Grace and A.E. Stoddart made three consecutive century opening stands. William Gunn of Nottinghamshire scored his only Test hundred, 102*, at Old Trafford, while Arthur Shrewsbury scored 106 at Lord's. Future England great Ranjitsinhji was one of the unfortunate bowlers as Australia set a new record team score of 843 against 'Oxford and Cambridge Past and Present' in Portsmouth.

Andrew Stoddart led England to a thrilling 3–2 victory on the 1894–1895 Ashes tour. Bobby Peel took the final wickets in the first Test victory at Sydney and the second at Melbourne and hit the winning runs in the final and deciding Test at the MCG. England's amazing victory at Sydney, by 10 runs, came after they had followed on with Lancashire's Albert Ward hitting 75 and 117 in the game. J.T. Brown scored 140 for England at Melbourne where England were set 297 to win. He reached 50 in 28 minutes and put on a then record 210 with Ward as England won by six wickets. Tom Richardson took 32 wickets in the Tests.

- England won all three Tests of the 1895/96 tour of South Africa by resounding margins. Lohmann was unplayable, taking 7 for 38 and 8 for 7 at Port Elizabeth and finishing with a hat trick. He took 9 for 28 and 3 for 43 at Johannesburg and 7 for 42 and 1 for 45 at Cape Town.

Having been overlooked for the first Test at Lord's, where Australian captain Harry Trott scored 143 and put on a record 210 with Syd Gregory (103), Shri Ranjitsinhji burst into Test cricket with 62 and 154 at Old Trafford in 1896. His magical batting and Tom Richardson's 13 for 244 were not enough to prevent Australia running out winners by 3 wickets however. Five English professionals went on 'strike' for more money before the Oval Test. Abel, Hayward and Richardson relented, but Gunn and Lohmann never played for England again. England won the series 2–1.

The Ashes were lost on Andrew Stoddart's 1897/98 tour, with Australia thumping England 4–1. Australian Joe Darling was the first batsmen to make 500 runs in a Test series, including 101 at Sydney, 178 at Adelaide and 160 in the final Sydney Test, where his hundred came up in 91 minutes. Stoddart's mother died just before the first Test and he was too distraught to play in either of the first two matches. Ranji, batting at number 7 after a throat infection, scored a brilliant 175 in the first Test and took England over 500 for the first time in a game won by 9 wickets but the Englishmen lost the next four heavily.

Lord Hawke's tourists in 1898/99 played and won two Tests in South Africa, with sometime Australian Albert Trott taking 17 wickets. Plum Warner carried his bat for 132 at Johannesburg in his maiden Test.

The 1899 series against Australia saw two significant developments. For the first time in England, five Tests were played rather than three, with Trent Bridge and Headingley being added to the "traditional" venues of Lord's, The Oval and Old Trafford. Also MCC and the counties appointed a selection committee for the first time. It comprised three active players: Lord Hawke, W.G. Grace and H.W. Bainbridge who was the captain of Warwickshire. Prior to this, England teams for home Tests had been chosen by the club on whose ground the match was to be played. The peerless Australian Victor Trumper dominated the series. He scored 1,500 runs on the tour, including 300 not out against Sussex and a breathtaking century in Australia's sole, but deciding, Test victory at Lords. W.G. Grace played his last Test at Trent Bridge. F.S. Jackson and Tom Hayward put on 185 at the Oval for the first wicket. England, scoring 576, forced Australia (352) to follow on, but the Australians played out the draw and with it retained the Ashes.

- 1900–1914: The "Golden Age"

The first Test series of the new century took place in Australia 1901–1902 and was won by Australia who came from one down to take the series 4–1. The England side was a private venture of Archie MacLaren (although the matches were all official Test matches). It was rather an attritional series of matches with only three centuries being scored and only one team innings over 400 (the first innings of England in the First Test at the SCG). Sydney Barnes made his debut for England and took 19 wickets in the first two Tests before being injured in the third and talking no further part in the series.

There was a home series against Australia in 1902 which was won by the Australians (2–1). In the drawn First Test at Edgbaston Australia were dismissed for 36 in their first innings (Wilfred Rhodes 7 for 17) but rain meant that the match was drawn. Rain also ruined the following match at Lord's. Sydney Barnes returned to the England team and had immediate success, taking seven wickets in the third Test at Sheffield (the only Test ever to be played there).

However England still lost the match. The final two Tests were amongst the most exciting of all time. A brilliant century by Trumper helped Australia to win the match at Old Trafford by three runs. England's batting throughout the series was modest with only one innings of over 300 and with only three centuries scored. The last of these was a match-winning innings in the final Test at The Oval by Gilbert Jessop, who went in at number seven in the second innings with England 48–5 and scored what was then the fastest century in Test cricket in 70 minutes, setting up an improbable England win by one wicket. The last wicket pair of Wilfred Rhodes and George Hirst nervelessly acquired the final fifteen runs needed for victory.

England toured Australia in 1903–1904, the first time that the MCC had been responsible for an England tour overseas. England regained The Ashes with a 3–2 series win under the captaincy of Plum Warner. In the first Test R.E.Foster made his Test debut and scored 287 in his first ever innings – the then highest ever Test score and a record that was to stand for a quarter of a century. Wilfred Rhodes took 15 wickets in England's second Test win at the MCG –a record that was to stand for thirty years. In the fifth Test England were dismissed for 61 in their first innings on a rain-affected pitch.

In 1905 Australia toured England and were beaten 2–0 with three matches drawn. Notable batting performances in the series included centuries by A.C. MacLaren, F.S. Jackson (2), Johnny Tyldesley (2) and C.B. Fry. B.J.T. Bosanquet, the inventor of the googly, took eight wickets in an Innings in the First Test.

In 1905–06 Plum Warner took an MCC team to South Africa for the first time and England were soundly beaten 4–1 in the series. England's batting faltered throughout the series with only one team innings in excess of 200 (successive innings of 184,190,148,160,295,196,198,160,187 and 130) and just one individual century (by F.L.Fane in the 3rd Test at the Wanderers). England's only win came at Newlands where the left-arm slow bowler Colin Blythe took eleven wickets in the match.

In 1907 there was a home three match Test series against South Africa which England, captained by R.E.Foster, won 1–0. Highlights included another sparkling innings by Gilbert Jessop who scored 93 at Lord's in a partnership of 145 for the sixth wicket with Len Braund who scored a century. There was another fine bowling performance by Blythe, who took 15 wickets at Headingley on a rain-affected match in a match that England won despite having been bowled out for 76 in their first innings.

In England's Test series in Australia in 1907–08 Australia won the first Test but England hit back well with a narrow win at the MCG in the 2nd Test in which Jack Hobbs made his England debut scoring 83 and 28. England were outplayed by Australia in the next three Tests and lost the series and the Ashes 4–1. England's batting was fragile throughout the series with only Gunn (2) and Hutchings scoring hundreds. The bowling relied on Jack Crawford), Arthur Fielder and Barnes, who took 79 wickets between them.

In a home series against Australia in 1909 England lost 2–1 (two draws) and no combination of players (England used 25 in total in the series) seemed to work. England failed to make 200 in an innings five times and there was only one individual century (by J. Sharp in the 3rd Test). The remarkable Colin Blythe delivered England's only victory by taking eleven wickets in the First Test at Edgbaston, but thereafter Australia, whilst never dominating the England attack, always had the edge.

England returned to South Africa in 1909–10 under H.D.G. Leveson-Gower, for a five match Test series and fared little better than on their first visit in 1905–06. The series was lost 3–2 but this disguises South Africa's superiority. The main highlight was Jack Hobbs first (of 15) Test century in the final Test at Newlands, he put on a then record 211 for the first wicket with Wilfred Rhodes. This was one of only two personal hundreds by England batsmen in the series. The bowling attack was weak – although the last of the great "lob" (underhand) bowlers George Simpson-Hayward had field days in the first three Test matches when he took a total of 21 wickets. Colin Blythe bowled England to a consolation win in the fifth Test with ten wickets in the match. Legspin dominated on the matting pitches, with the ball often bouncing chest high. Vogler took 29 wickets for the home side and Faulkner 29.

England toured Australia in 1911/12 under Plum Warner, but Johnny Douglas took over the captaincy when Warner fell ill prior to the first Test. Despite losing that first match at Sydney, a side which boasted Jack Hobbs, Frank Woolley, Sydney Barnes and Wilfred Rhodes hit back to take the next four Tests in style. Frank Foster and Barnes dominated with the ball, sharing 66 wickets, while Hobbs, Rhodes and Woolley recorded centuries. Hobbs and Rhodes shared opening stands of 147 at Adelaide and a then record 323 at Melbourne in the next Test where Barnes dismissed Bardsley, Kelleway, Hill and Armstrong for 3 runs in his opening spell. Later in the game, when the crowd barracked Barnes for deliberating over a field setting, he threw the ball down in disgust and refused to continue until order was restored. Frank Woolley also hit 305* in 205 minutes in a tour game against Tasmania.

The 1912 home season saw a unique experiment with a 9 Test triangular tournament involving South Africa and Australia but it was an idea ahead of its time and was not repeated. C.B. Fry of Sussex captained the team against Syd Gregory of Australia and Frank Mitchell of South Africa. Jack Hobbs scored 107 against Australia at Lords in a rain ruined game. The Australia v South Africa match, at Lord's, was notable for a visit by King George V, the first time a reigning monarch had watched Test cricket. Barnes took 34 wickets in his 3 Tests against the South Africans.

England's 1913/14 tour of South Africa was the last before the onset of World War I, and England dominated the rubber, winning 4–0. Syd Barnes was once again unplayable, taking 49 wickets in four Tests before boycotting the last in a row over his wife's accommodation. Only Herbie Taylor resisted for the home side, with skilful backfoot defence on the matting pitches, scoring 508 runs at 50.8.

- 1920s

England resumed their Test cricket after World War I with a tour of Australia in 1920/21 under Johnny Douglas. After the ravages of the war it was little surprise when England went down to a series of crushing defeats, the first 5–0 whitewash. Six Australians scored hundreds while Mailey spun out 36 English batsmen. Things were no better when Warwick Armstrong's men toured England in 1921. Australian fast bowlers Gregory and McDonald battered the English batsmen with a succession of bouncers and Jack Hobbs missed most of the season with first a leg injury then appendicitis. England used 30 players in all. Only one Australian made a century as opposed to 3 for England – A. C. "Jack" Russell scoring 101 and 102* and Phil Mead 182* – but Australia's 3–0 victory made it 8 Ashes defeats in succession.

England resumed the winning habit on the 1922/23 tour of South Africa, under F.T. Mann, winning a pulsating rubber 2 – 1. England lost the first Test but scraped to victory in the next, at Cape Town, by one wicket. Phil Mead scored 181 at Kingsmead, Durban, to ensure a draw and they won the fifth and final match, also at Durban, thanks to Jack Russell's twin centuries in his final Test. This dominance was underlined in England in 1924 with a 3–0 for England.

Hopes that the Ashes might be regained were dashed on the 1924/25 tour down under however, Australia thrashing England 4–1, although England scored 8 centuries to Australia's 6. Herbert Sutcliffe scored 734 runs at 81.56 and Maurice Tate broke Mailey's Ashes record with 38 wickets, bowling 2,528 balls in the Tests. England's only victory came at Melbourne, by an innings, after Captain Arthur Gilligan won the toss for the only time. It was England's first Ashes Test win in 12 years.

England drew the first four Tests of the 1926 Ashes series and so the series rested on the Oval Test, for which Percy Chapman replaced Arthur Carr as captain and both the 48-year-old Rhodes and 21-year-old Larwood were selected. Hobbs and Sutcliffe scored centuries and Australia lost by 289 runs. The South African team proved stronger than before however and drew the 1927/28 series 2–2.

A fourth team was, at last, introduced to Test cricket when the West Indies took their bow in 1928. England won each of the three Tests by an innings, Freeman taking 22 wickets, and a view was expressed in the press that their elevation had proved a mistake although 'electric heels' Learie Constantine did the double on the tour. The England team at this period was as strong as it has ever been and Australia were dispatched 4–1 on the 1928/29 Ashes tour. Hammond scored 44, 28, 251, 200, 32, 119*, 177, 38 and 16 – a total of 905 runs, a new record. Percy Chapman captained the team but barely played again.

England, under J. C. White and Arthur Carr, beat South Africa 2–0 at home in 1929 with Herbert Sutcliffe scoring a hundred in each innings at the Oval Bizarrely there were two concurrent England tours in 1929/30, one to New Zealand and one to the West Indies. Surrey paceman Maurice Allom took four wickets in five balls in New Zealand's maiden Test match, including a hat trick, and his 8 for 65 swept England to victory in Christchurch by 8 wickets with the three later Tests drawn. At the same time another England team were drawing 1–1 in the West Indies under F. S. G. Calthorpe. Forty-year-old Patsy Hendren made 1,765 runs on this tour and Andy Sandham scored 325 at Kingston (out of England's 849) in his final Test. The 'black Bradman' George Headley followed twin centuries at Georgetown with 223 in the same Kingston game.

- 1930s

The 21-year-old Don Bradman dominated the 1930 Ashes series in England, scoring 974 runs in his seven Test innings. He scored 254 at Lord's, 334 at Headingley, when Chapman stuck to attacking fields all day, and 232 at the Oval. Australia regained the Ashes. Harold Larwood took only four wickets in the series although K. S. Duleepsinhji made 173 at Lord's on debut.

England played five Tests in South Africa on the 1930/31 tour. Chasing 240 to win the first Test at the Old Wanderers ground in Johannesburg they were bowled out by E. P. Nupen, a master on the matting wicket, and drew the next four.

New Zealand played their first Test in England in 1931 and their strong performance at Lord's led the authorities to arrange another two that summer, one of which England won. India played their first Test in England in 1932 at Lords, reducing England to 19 for 3 on the first morning before losing a competitive match when they were bowled out for 187 chasing 346.

Bill Woodfull evades a Bodyline ball. Note the number of leg-side fielders.

Before the 1932–3 tour to Australia, England had become used to the prolific run-scoring of Don Bradman. The England captain, Surrey's Douglas Jardine chose to develop the already existing leg theory into fast leg theory, or bodyline, as a tactic to stop Bradman. Fast leg theory involved bowling fast balls directly at the batsman's body, and Jardine had two very fast accurate bowlers, Harold Larwood and Bill Voce to bowl them. The batsman would need to defend himself, and if he touched the ball with the bat, he risked being caught by one of a large number of fielders placed on the leg side.

England won the series and the Ashes 4–1. But complaints about the Bodyline tactic caused crowd disruption on the tour, and threats of diplomatic action from the Australian Cricket Board, which during the tour sent the following cable to the Marylebone Cricket Club in London:

Bodyline bowling assumed such proportions as to menace best interests of game, making protection of body by batsmen the main consideration. Causing intensely bitter feeling between players as well as injury. In our opinion is unsportsmanlike. Unless stopped at once likely to upset friendly relations existing between Australia and England.

Later, Jardine was removed from the captaincy and the laws of cricket changed so that no more than one fast ball aimed at the body was permitted per over, and having more than two fielders behind square leg were banned.

England won two Tests on the 1933/34 tour of India, the first ever Tests held in the sub continent. England won by nine wickets at Bombay's Gymkhana ground with Bryan Valentine scoring 136 in his first Test innings. Morris Nichols and E. W. "Nobby" Clark bowled so many bouncers at the Indian batsman that they wore solar topees instead of caps to protect themselves from the ball as much as the sun. Naoomal Jeoomal top edged a Clark bouncer into his head in the third Test, was unable to continue and didn't bat in the second innings.

Australia won the first Test of the 1934 Ashes series by 238 runs at Trent Bridge. Clarrie Grimmett took 25 wickets in the series, and Bill O'Reilly 28 as England were spun to defeat. Bradman made 758 runs in the Tests and 2020 on the tour, with Stan McCabe making 2078. Patsy Hendren(132) and Maurice Leyland (153) ensured a draw at Old Trafford and England did manage a rare Test win over Australia at Lord's with Hedley Verity taking 14 wickets in a day and 15 in the match. Bradman (304) and Ponsford (181) put on 388 at Headingley and then 451 at the Oval where England lost by a massive 562 runs. Ponsford scored 266 in his last Test. Nobby Clark bowled some 'leg theory' against the Australians, with little success. Bill Voce took 8 for 66 for Notts against the Australians but withdrew from the attack with a 'leg injury' after Woodfall raised discrete objections.

England toured the West Indies in 1934/5 and showed the folly of sending a weakened team as they lost the rubber 2–1 with George Headley scoring 270 not out in the 4th Test at Sabina Park. South Africa won on English soil for the first time, taking the 5 Test series 1–0 in 1935 with a victory at Lord's by 157 runs thanks to Bruce Mitchell's 164 and Jock Cameron's quickfire 90. Cameron died at 30, of enteric fever, soon after returning home from this tour.

India used 22 players in three Tests in England in 1936. A then record 588 runs were scored on the second day of the Old Trafford Test and England too experimented with their team and took the rubber 2–0.

The 1936/37 Ashes tour, under Gubby Allen, was a titanic struggle. England, helped by rain freshening the pitch, won by 322 runs in Brisbane and an innings in Sydney where Wally Hammond scored 271 not out. Bill Voce was their spearhead, taking 17 wickets in these two games. Bradman added a record 346 for the sixth wicket with Jack Fingleton at Melbourne and followed that with 212 at Adelaide where his team leveled the score at 2–2. Bradman, McCabe and Badcock all scored hundreds in the decider at Melbourne and Australian took the series 3–2.

England beat New Zealand 1–0 in a three Test rubber in 1937. Tom Goddard took 6 for 29 in bowling out the visitors for 134 at the Old Trafford Test as they chased 265 to win. Jack Cowie had taken 6 for 67 for New Zealand and 10 in the match. Len Hutton scored a century after having begun his England career with 0 and 1 at Lords. Prospective tours of South Africa and West Indies fell through in the winter of 1937/38.

The 1938 Ashes series was a high scoring affair. Hutton, Barnett, Paynter (216*) and Compton made hundreds at Trent Bridge with the Australians scoring three including Stan McCabe's brilliant 232.

Hammond scored 240 in the Lord's Test while Bill Brown made a double ton and Bradman a match saving century for Australia. Old Trafford fell victim to the rain and Australia retained the Ashes with a win at Headingley, thanks to Bradman's century and 10 wickets for O'Reilly and 7 for Fleetwood-Smith. England won the final Test at the Oval thanks to a record Test score of 903 – 7 dec and Len Hutton's world record of 364 in 13 hours, 17 minutes. Bradman, whose score of 334 had been surpassed, was the first to congratulate the 22-year-old Yorkshireman. Maurice Leyland made 187 and the elegant Joe Hardstaff 169 not out. Australia subsided to 201 and 123, batting 2 short, and England won by an innings and 579.

Paul Gibb scored 93 and 106 on debut at Johannesburg on England's 1938/39 tour. England scored 11 centuries in the series and South Africa 6. Paynter scored 117 and 100 in the first Test and 243 in the third at Durban. England, 1–0, in the series, returned to Durban to play a deciding 'timeless' Test to the finish. It was abandoned as a draw after 10 days as England had to catch the train to catch the boat home. Needing 696 to win they were, incredibly, 654 for 5, Gibb having scored 120, Hammond 140 and Edrich 219. A record 1981 runs were scored, and the concept of timeless Tests was abandoned.

The three Tests between England and the West Indies in 1939 were the last before the Second World War, although a team for an MCC tour of India was selected more in hope than expectation of the matches being played. Len Hutton and Denis Compton, leaders of the bright new batting generation, scored hundreds at Lords where the brilliant George Headley scored a ton in each innings. Hammond became the first fielder to hold 100 Test catches at Old Trafford. England took the series 1–0 as the war clouds loomed over Europe.

CHAPTER FOUR

What Is Cricket ?

- What Is Cricket ?

Cricket is a bat-and-ball game played between two teams of eleven players on a field at the centre of which is a 22-yard (20-metre) pitch with a wicket at each end, each comprising two bails balanced on three stumps. The game proceeds when a player on the fielding team, called the bowler, "bowls" (propels) the ball from one end of the pitch towards the wicket at the other end. The batting side's players score runs by striking the bowled ball with a bat and running between the wickets, while the bowling side tries to prevent this by keeping the ball within the field and getting it to either wicket, and dismiss each batter (so they are "out"). Means of dismissal include being bowled, when the ball hits the stumps and dislodges the bails, and by the fielding side either catching a hit ball before it touches the ground, or hitting a wicket with the ball before a batter can cross the crease line in front of the wicket to complete a run. When ten batters have been dismissed, the innings ends and the teams swap roles. The game is adjudicated by two umpires, aided by a third umpire and match referee in international matches.

Forms of cricket range from Twenty20, with each team batting for a single innings of 20 overs and the game generally lasting three hours, to Test matches played over five days. Traditionally cricketers play in all-white kit, but in limited overs cricket they wear club or team colours. In addition to the basic kit, some players wear protective gear to prevent injury caused by the ball, which is a hard, solid spheroid made of compressed leather with a slightly raised sewn seam enclosing a cork core layered with tightly wound string.

The earliest reference to cricket is in South East England in the mid-16th century. It spread globally with the expansion of the British Empire, with the first international matches in the second half of the 19th century. The game's governing body is the International Cricket Council (ICC), which has over 100 members, twelve of which are full members who play Test matches. The game's rules, the Laws of Cricket, are maintained by Marylebone Cricket Club (MCC) in London. The sport is followed primarily in South Asia, Australasia, the United Kingdom, southern Africa and the West Indies.Women's cricket, which is organised and played separately, has also achieved international standard. The most successful side playing international cricket is Australia, which has won seven One Day International trophies, including five World Cups, more than any other country and has been the top-rated Test side more than any other country.

- History of cricket to 1725

A medieval "club ball" game involving an underhand bowl towards a batter. Ball catchers are shown positioning themselves to catch a ball. Detail from the Canticles of Holy Mary, 13th century.

Cricket is one of many games in the "club ball" sphere that basically involve hitting a ball with a hand-held implement; others include baseball (which shares many similarities with cricket, both belonging in the more specific bat-and-ball games category), golf, hockey, tennis, squash, badminton and table tennis. In cricket's case, a key difference is the existence of a solid target structure, the wicket (originally, it is thought, a "wicket gate" through which sheep were herded), that the batter must defend. The cricket historian Harry Altham identified three "groups" of "club ball" games: the "hockey group", in which the ball is driven to and fro between two targets (the goals); the "golf group", in which the ball is driven towards an undefended target (the hole); and the "cricket group", in which "the ball is aimed at a mark (the wicket) and driven away from it".

It is generally believed that cricket originated as a children's game in the south-eastern counties of England, sometime during the medieval period.Although there are claims for prior dates, the earliest definite reference to cricket being played comes from evidence given at a court case in Guildford in January 1597 (Old Style), equating to January 1598 in the modern calendar. The case concerned ownership of a certain plot of land and the court heard the testimony of a 59-year-old coroner, John Derrick, who gave witness that.

Being a scholler in the ffree schoole of Guldeford hee and diverse of his fellows did runne and play there at creckett and other plaies.

Given Derrick's age, it was about half a century earlier when he was at school and so it is certain that cricket was being played c. 1550 by boys in Surrey. The view that it was originally a children's game is reinforced by Randle Cotgrave's 1611 English-French dictionary in which he defined the noun "crosse" as "the crooked staff wherewith boys play at cricket" and the verb form "crosser" as "to play at cricket".

One possible source for the sport's name is the Old English word "cryce" (or "cricc") meaning a crutch or staff. In Samuel Johnson's Dictionary, he derived cricket from "cryce, Saxon, a stick". In Old French, the word "criquet" seems to have meant a kind of club or stick. Given the strong medieval trade connections between south-east England and the County of Flanders when the latter belonged to the Duchy of Burgundy, the name may have been derived from the Middle Dutch (in use in Flanders at the time) "krick"(-e), meaning a stick (crook). Another possible source is the Middle Dutch word "krickstoel", meaning a long low stool used for kneeling in church and which resembled the long low wicket with two stumps used in early cricket. According to Heiner Gillmeister, a European language expert of Bonn University, "cricket" derives from the Middle Dutch phrase for hockey, met de (krik ket)sen (i.e., "with the stick chase"). Gillmeister has suggested that not only the name but also the sport itself may be of Flemish origin.

- Growth of amateur and professional cricket in England

Evolution of the cricket bat. The original "hockey stick" (left) evolved into the straight bat from c. 1760 when pitched delivery bowling began.

Although the main object of the game has always been to score the most runs, the early form of cricket differed from the modern game in certain key technical aspects; the North American variant of cricket known as wicket retained many of these aspects. The ball was bowled underarm by the bowler and along the ground towards a batter armed with a bat that in shape resembled a hockey stick; the batter defended a low, two-stump wicket; and runs were called notches because the scorers recorded them by notching tally sticks.

In 1611, the year Cotgrave's dictionary was published, ecclesiastical court records at Sidlesham in Sussex state that two parishioners, Bartholomew Wyatt and Richard Latter, failed to attend church on Easter Sunday because they were playing cricket. They were fined 12d each and ordered to do penance.This is the earliest mention of adult participation in cricket and it was around the same time that the earliest known organised inter-parish or village match was played – at Chevening, Kent. In 1624, a player called Jasper Vinall died after he was accidentally struck on the head during a match between two parish teams in Sussex.

Cricket remained a low-key local pursuit for much of the 17th century. It is known, through numerous references found in the records of ecclesiastical court cases, to have been proscribed at times by the Puritans before and during the Commonwealth. The problem was nearly always the issue of Sunday play as the Puritans considered cricket to be "profane" if played on the Sabbath, especially if large crowds or gambling were involved.

According to the social historian Derek Birley, there was a "great upsurge of sport after the Restoration" in 1660. Gambling on sport became a problem significant enough for Parliament to pass the 1664 Gambling Act, limiting stakes to £100 which was, in any case, a colossal sum exceeding the annual income of 99% of the population. Along with prizefighting, horse racing and blood sports, cricket was perceived to be a gambling sport.Rich patrons made matches for high stakes, forming teams in which they engaged the first professional players.By the end of the century, cricket had developed into a major sport that was spreading throughout England and was already being taken abroad by English mariners and colonisers – the earliest reference to cricket overseas is dated 1676. A 1697 newspaper report survives of "a great cricket match" played in Sussex "for fifty guineas apiece" – this is the earliest known contest that is generally considered a First Class match.

- The patrons, and other players from the social class known as the "gentry", began to classify themselves as "amateurs" to establish a clear distinction from the professionals, who were invariably members of the working class, even to the point of having separate changing and dining facilities. The gentry, including such high-ranking nobles as the Dukes of Richmond, exerted their honour code of noblesse oblige to claim rights of leadership in any sporting contests they took part in, especially as it was necessary for them to play alongside their "social inferiors" if they were to win their bets. In time, a perception took hold that the typical amateur who played in first-class cricket, until 1962 when amateurism was abolished, was someone with a public school education who had then gone to one of Cambridge or Oxford University – society insisted that such people were "officers and gentlemen" whose destiny was to provide leadership. In a purely financial sense, the cricketing amateur would theoretically claim expenses for playing while his professional counterpart played under contract and was paid a wage or match fee; in practice, many amateurs claimed more than actual expenditure and the derisive term "shamateur" was coined to describe the practice.

- The Young Cricketer, 1768

The game underwent major development in the 18th century to become England's national sport.Its success was underwritten by the twin necessities of patronage and betting. Cricket was prominent in London as early as 1707 and, in the middle years of the century, large crowds flocked to matches on the Artillery Ground in Finsbury. The single wicket form of the sport attracted huge crowds and wagers to match, its popularity peaking in the 1748 season. Bowling underwent an evolution around 1760 when bowlers began to pitch the ball instead of rolling or skimming it towards the batter. This caused a revolution in bat design because, to deal with the bouncing ball, it was necessary to introduce the modern straight bat in place of the old "hockey stick" shape.

The Hambledon Club was founded in the 1760s and, for the next twenty years until the formation of Marylebone Cricket Club (MCC) and the opening of Lord's Old Ground in 1787, Hambledon was both the game's greatest club and its focal point. MCC quickly became the sport's premier club and the custodian of the Laws of Cricket. New Laws introduced in the latter part of the 18th century included the three stump wicket and leg before wicket (lbw).

The 19th century saw underarm bowling superseded by first roundarm and then overarm bowling. Both developments were controversial.Organisation of the game at county level led to the creation of the county clubs, starting with Sussex in 1839. In December 1889, the eight leading county clubs formed the official County Championship, which began in 1890.

The most famous player of the 19th century was W. G. Grace, who started his long and influential career in 1865. It was especially during the career of Grace that the distinction between amateurs and professionals became blurred by the existence of players like him who were nominally amateur but, in terms of their financial gain, de facto professional. Grace himself was said to have been paid more money for playing cricket than any professional.

The last two decades before the First World War have been called the "Golden Age of cricket". It is a nostalgic name prompted by the collective sense of loss resulting from the war, but the period did produce some great players and memorable matches, especially as organised competition at county and Test level developed.

- Cricket becomes an international sport

In 1844, the first-ever international match took place between the United States and Canada. In 1859, a team of English players went to North America on the first overseas tour. Meanwhile, the British Empire had been instrumental in spreading the game overseas and by the middle of the 19th century it had become well established in Australia, the Caribbean, India, Pakistan, New Zealand, North America and South Africa.

In 1862, an English team made the first tour of Australia. The first Australian team to travel overseas consisted of Aboriginal stockmen who toured England in 1868. The first One Day International match was played on 5 January 1971 between Australia and England at the Melbourne Cricket Ground.

In 1876–77, an England team took part in what was retrospectively recognised as the first-ever Test match at the Melbourne Cricket Ground against Australia. The rivalry between England and Australia gave birth to The Ashes in 1882, and this has remained Test cricket's most famous contest. Test cricket began to expand in 1888–89 when South Africa played England.

- World cricket in the 20th century

The inter-war years were dominated by Australia's Don Bradman, statistically the greatest Test batter of all time. Test cricket continued to expand during the 20th century with the addition of the West Indies (1928),

New Zealand (1930) and India (1932) before the Second World War and then Pakistan (1952), Sri Lanka (1982), Zimbabwe (1992), Bangladesh (2000), Ireland and Afghanistan (both 2018) in the post-war period. South Africa was banned from international cricket from 1970 to 1992 as part of the apartheid boycott.

- The rise of limited overs cricket

Cricket entered a new era in 1963 when English counties introduced the limited overs variant. As it was sure to produce a result, limited overs cricket was lucrative and the number of matches increased. The first Limited Overs International was played in 1971 and the governing International Cricket Council (ICC), seeing its potential, staged the first limited overs Cricket World Cup in 1975. In the 21st century, a new limited overs form, Twenty20, made an immediate impact. On 22 June 2017, Afghanistan and Ireland became the 11th and 12th ICC full members, enabling them to play Test cricket.

- A typical cricket field.

In cricket, the rules of the game are specified in a code called The Laws of Cricket (hereinafter called "the Laws") which has a global remit. There are 42 Laws (always written with a capital "L"). The earliest known version of the code was drafted in 1744 and, since 1788, it has been owned and maintained by its custodian, the Marylebone Cricket Club (MCC) in London.

- Playing area

Cricket is a bat-and-ball game played on a cricket field between two teams of eleven players each. The field is usually circular or oval in shape and the edge of the playing area is marked by a boundary, which may be a fence, part of the stands, a rope, a painted line or a combination of these; the boundary must if possible be marked along its entire length.

In the approximate centre of the field is a rectangular pitch (see image, below) on which a wooden target called a wicket is sited at each end; the wickets are placed 22 yards (20 m) apart. The pitch is a flat surface 10 feet (3.0 m) wide, with very short grass that tends to be worn away as the game progresses (cricket can also be played on artificial surfaces, notably matting). Each wicket is made of three wooden stumps topped by two bails.

- Cricket pitch and creases

As illustrated above, the pitch is marked at each end with four white painted lines: a bowling crease, a popping crease and two return creases. The three stumps are aligned centrally on the bowling crease, which is eight feet eight inches long. The popping crease is drawn four feet in front of the bowling crease and parallel to it; although it is drawn as a twelve-foot line (six feet either side of the wicket), it is, in fact, unlimited in length. The return creases are drawn at right angles to the popping crease so that they intersect the ends of the bowling crease; each return crease is drawn as an eight-foot line, so that it extends four feet behind the bowling crease, but is also, in fact, unlimited in length.

Before a match begins, the team captains (who are also players) toss a coin to decide which team will bat first and so take the first innings. Innings is the term used for each phase of play in the match.In each innings, one team bats, attempting to score runs, while the other team bowls and fields the ball, attempting to restrict the scoring and dismiss the batters. When the first innings ends, the teams change roles; there can be two to four innings depending upon the type of match. A match with four scheduled innings is played over three to five days; a match with two scheduled innings is usually completed in a single day. During an innings, all eleven members of the fielding team take the field, but usually only two members of the batting team are on the field at any given time. The exception to this is if a batter has any type of illness or injury restricting his or her ability to run, in this case the batter is allowed a runner who can run between the wickets when the batter hits a scoring run or runs,though this does not apply in international cricket. The order of batters is usually announced just before the match, but it can be varied.

The main objective of each team is to score more runs than their opponents but, in some forms of cricket, it is also necessary to dismiss all of the opposition batters in their final innings in order to win the match, which would otherwise be drawn. If the team batting last is all out having scored fewer runs than their opponents, they are said to have "lost by n runs" (where n is the difference between the aggregate number of runs scored by the teams). If the team that bats last scores enough runs to win, it is said to have "won by n wickets", where n is the number of wickets left to fall. For example, a team that passes its opponents‘ total having lost six wickets (i.e., six of their batters have been dismissed) have won the match "by four wickets".

In a two-innings-a-side match, one team's combined first and second innings total may be less than the other side's first innings total. The team with the greater score is then said to have "won by an innings and n runs", and does not need to bat again: n is the difference between the two teams' aggregate scores. If the team batting last is all out, and both sides have scored the same number of runs, then the match is a tie; this result is quite rare in matches of two innings a side with only 62 happening in first-class matches from the earliest known instance in 1741 until January 2017. In the traditional form of the game, if the time allotted for the match expires before either side can win, then the game is declared a draw.

If the match has only a single innings per side, then a maximum number of overs applies to each innings. Such a match is called a "limited overs" or "one-day" match, and the side scoring more runs wins regardless of the number of wickets lost, so that a draw cannot occur. In some cases, ties are broken by having each team bat for a one-over innings known as a Super Over; subsequent Super Overs may be played if the first Super Over ends in a tie. If this kind of match is temporarily interrupted by bad weather, then a complex mathematical formula, known as the Duckworth–Lewis–Stern method after its developers, is often used to recalculate a new target score. A one-day match can also be declared a "no-result" if fewer than a previously agreed number of overs have been bowled by either team, in circumstances that make normal resumption of play impossible; for example, wet weather.

In all forms of cricket, the umpires can abandon the match if bad light or rain makes it impossible to continue. There have been instances of entire matches, even Test matches scheduled to be played over five days, being lost to bad weather without a ball being bowled: for example, the third Test of the 1970/71 series in Australia.

- Innings

The innings (ending with 's' in both singular and plural form) is the term used for each phase of play during a match. Depending on the type of match being played, each team has either one or two innings. Sometimes all eleven members of the batting side take a turn to bat but, for various reasons, an innings can end before they have all done so. The innings terminates if the batting team is "all out", a term defined by the Laws: "at the fall of a wicket or the retirement of a batter, further balls remain to be bowled but no further batter is available to come in". In this situation, one of the batters has not been dismissed and is termed not out; this is because he has no partners left and there must always be two active batters while the innings is in progress.

- An innings may end early while there are still two not out batters

the batting team's captain may declare the innings closed even though some of his players have not had a turn to bat: this is a tactical decision by the captain, usually because he believes his team have scored sufficient runs and need time to dismiss the opposition in their innings

the set number of overs (i.e., in a limited overs match) have been bowled

the match has ended prematurely due to bad weather or running out of time

in the final innings of the match, the batting side has reached its target and won the game.

- Overs

The Laws state that, throughout an innings, "the ball shall be bowled from each end alternately in overs of 6 balls". The name "over" came about because the umpire calls "Over!" when six balls have been bowled. At this point, another bowler is deployed at the other end, and the fielding side changes ends while the batters do not. A bowler cannot bowl two successive overs, although a bowler can (and usually does) bowl alternate overs, from the same end, for several overs which are termed a "spell". The batters do not change ends at the end of the over, and so the one who was non-striker is now the striker and vice versa. The umpires also change positions so that the one who was at "square leg" now stands behind the wicket at the non-striker's end and vice versa.

- Clothing and equipment

English cricketer W. G. Grace "taking guard" in 1883. His pads and bat are very similar to those used today. The gloves have evolved somewhat. Many modern players use more defensive equipment than were available to Grace, most notably helmets and arm guards.

The wicket-keeper (a specialised fielder behind the batter) and the batters wear protective gear because of the hardness of the ball, which can be delivered at speeds of more than 145 kilometres per hour (90 mph) and presents a major health and safety concern. Protective clothing includes pads (designed to protect the knees and shins), batting gloves or wicket-keeper's gloves for the hands, a safety helmet for the head and a box for male players inside the trousers (to protect the crotch area). Some batters wear additional padding inside their shirts and trousers such as thigh pads, arm pads, rib protectors and shoulder pads. The only fielders allowed to wear protective gear are those in positions very close to the batter (i.e., if they are alongside or in front of him), but they cannot wear gloves or external leg guards.

Subject to certain variations, on-field clothing generally includes a collared shirt with short or long sleeves; long trousers; woolen pullover (if needed); cricket cap (for fielding) or a safety helmet; and spiked shoes or boots to increase traction. The kit is traditionally all white and this remains the case in Test and first-class cricket but, in limited overs cricket, team colours are worn instead.

- Bat and ball

Two types of cricket ball, both of the same size:

i) A used white ball. White balls are mainly used in limited overs cricket, especially in matches played at night, under floodlights (left).

ii) A used red ball. Red balls are used in Test cricket, first-class cricket and some other forms of cricket (right).

The essence of the sport is that a bowler delivers (i.e., bowls) the ball from his or her end of the pitch towards the batter who, armed with a bat, is "on strike" at the other end (see next sub-section: Basic gameplay).

The bat is made of wood, usually Salix alba (white willow), and has the shape of a blade topped by a cylindrical handle. The blade must not be more than 4.25 inches (10.8 cm) wide and the total length of the bat not more than 38 inches (97 cm). There is no standard for the weight, which is usually between 2 lb 7 oz and 3 lb (1.1 and 1.4 kg).

The ball is a hard leather-seamed spheroid, with a circumference of 9 inches (23 cm). The ball has a "seam": six rows of stitches attaching the leather shell of the ball to the string and cork interior. The seam on a new ball is prominent and helps the bowler propel it in a less predictable manner. During matches, the quality of the ball deteriorates to a point where it is no longer usable; during the course of this deterioration, its behaviour in flight will change and can influence the outcome of the match. Players will, therefore, attempt to modify the ball's behaviour by modifying its physical properties. Polishing the ball and wetting it with sweat or saliva is legal, even when the polishing is deliberately done on one side only to increase the ball's swing through the air, but the acts of rubbing other substances into the ball, scratching the surface or picking at the seam are illegal ball tampering.

- Player roles

Basic gameplay: bowler to batter

During normal play, thirteen players and two umpires are on the field. Two of the players are batters and the rest are all eleven members of the fielding team. The other nine players in the batting team are off the field in the pavilion. The image with overlay below shows what is happening when a ball is being bowled and which of the personnel are on or close to the pitch.

- Return crease

In the photo, the two batters (3 & 8; wearing yellow) have taken position at each end of the pitch (6). Three members of the fielding team (4, 10 & 11; wearing dark blue) are in shot. One of the two umpires (1; wearing white hat) is stationed behind the wicket (2) at the bowler's (4) end of the pitch. The bowler (4) is bowling the ball (5) from his end of the pitch to the batter at the other end who is called the "striker". The other batter (3) at the bowling end is called the "non-striker". The wicket-keeper (10), who is a specialist, is positioned behind the striker's wicket (9) and behind him stands one of the fielders in a position called "first slip" (11). While the bowler and the first slip are wearing conventional kit only, the two batters and the wicket-keeper are wearing protective gear including safety helmets, padded gloves and leg guards (pads).

While the umpire (1) in shot stands at the bowler's end of the pitch, his colleague stands in the outfield, usually in or near the fielding position called "square leg", so that he is in line with the popping crease (7) at the striker's end of the pitch. The bowling crease (not numbered) is the one on which the wicket is located between the return creases (12). The bowler (4) intends to hit the wicket (9) with the ball (5) or, at least, to prevent the striker (8) from scoring runs. The striker (8) intends, by using his bat, to defend his wicket and, if possible, to hit the ball away from the pitch in order to score runs.

Some players are skilled in both batting and bowling, or as either or these as well as wicket-keeping, so are termed all-rounders. Bowlers are classified according to their style, generally as fast bowlers, seam bowlers or spinners. Batters are classified according to whether they are right-handed or left-handed.

- Fielding

Of the eleven fielders, three are in shot in the image above. The other eight are elsewhere on the field, their positions determined on a tactical basis by the captain or the bowler. Fielders often change position between deliveries, again as directed by the captain or bowler.

If a fielder is injured or becomes ill during a match, a substitute is allowed to field instead of him, but the substitute cannot bowl or act as a captain, except in the case of concussion substitutes in international cricket. The substitute leaves the field when the injured player is fit to return. The Laws of Cricket were updated in 2017 to allow substitutes to act as wicket-keepers.

- Bowling and dismissal

Glenn McGrath of Australia holds the world record for most wickets in the Cricket World Cup.

Most bowlers are considered specialists in that they are selected for the team because of their skill as a bowler, although some are all-rounders and even specialist batters bowl occasionally. The specialists bowl several times during an innings but may not bowl two overs consecutively. If the captain wants a bowler to "change ends", another bowler must temporarily fill in so that the change is not immediate.

A bowler reaches his delivery stride by means of a "run-up" and an over is deemed to have begun when the bowler starts his run-up for the first delivery of that over, the ball then being "in play".

Fast bowlers, needing momentum, take a lengthy run up while bowlers with a slow delivery take no more than a couple of steps before bowling. The fastest bowlers can deliver the ball at a speed of over 145 kilometres per hour (90 mph) and they sometimes rely on sheer speed to try to defeat the batter, who is forced to react very quickly.

Other fast bowlers rely on a mixture of speed and guile by making the ball seam or swing (i.e. curve) in flight. This type of delivery can deceive a batter into miscuing his shot, for example, so that the ball just touches the edge of the bat and can then be "caught behind" by the wicket-keeper or a slip fielder. At the other end of the bowling scale is the spin bowler who bowls at a relatively slow pace and relies entirely on guile to deceive the batter. A spinner will often "buy his wicket" by "tossing one up" (in a slower, steeper parabolic path) to lure the batter into making a poor shot. The batter has to be very wary of such deliveries as they are often "flighted" or spun so that the ball will not behave quite as he expects and he could be "trapped" into getting himself out. In between the pacemen and the spinners are the medium paced seamers who rely on persistent accuracy to try to contain the rate of scoring and wear down the batter's concentration.

There are nine ways in which a batter can be dismissed: five relatively common and four extremely rare. The common forms of dismissal are bowled, caught, leg before wicket (lbw), run out and stumped. Rare methods are hit wicket,hit the ball twice, obstructing the field and timed out. The Laws state that the fielding team, usually the bowler in practice, must appeal for a dismissal before the umpire can give his decision. If the batter is out, the umpire raises a forefinger and says "Out!"; otherwise, he will shake his head and say "Not out".There is, effectively, a tenth method of dismissal, retired out, which is not an on-field dismissal as such but rather a retrospective one for which no fielder is credited.

- Batting, runs and extras

The directions in which a right-handed batter, facing down the page, intends to send the ball when playing various cricketing shots. The diagram for a left-handed batter is a mirror image of this one.

Batters take turns to bat via a batting order which is decided beforehand by the team captain and presented to the umpires, though the order remains flexible when the captain officially nominates the team. Substitute batters are generally not allowed, except in the case of concussion substitutes in international cricket.

In order to begin batting the batter first adopts a batting stance. Standardly, this involves adopting a slight crouch with the feet pointing across the front of the wicket, looking in the direction of the bowler, and holding the bat so it passes over the feet and so its tip can rest on the ground near to the toes of the back foot.

A skilled batter can use a wide array of "shots" or "strokes" in both defensive and attacking mode. The idea is to hit the ball to the best effect with the flat surface of the bat's blade. If the ball touches the side of the bat it is called an "edge". The batter does not have to play a shot and can allow the ball to go through to the wicketkeeper. Equally, he does not have to attempt a run when he hits the ball with his bat. Batters do not always seek to hit the ball as hard as possible, and a good player can score runs just by making a deft stroke with a turn of the wrists or by simply "blocking" the ball but directing it away from fielders so that he has time to take a run. A wide variety of shots are played, the batter's repertoire including strokes named according to the style of swing and the direction aimed: e.g., "cut", "drive", "hook", "pull".

The batter on strike (i.e. the "striker") must prevent the ball hitting the wicket, and try to score runs by hitting the ball with his bat so that he and his partner have time to run from one end of the pitch to the other before the fielding side can return the ball. To register a run, both runners must touch the ground behind the popping crease with either their bats or their bodies (the batters carry their bats as they run). Each completed run increments the score of both the team and the striker.

- Sachin Tendulkar is the only player to have scored one hundred international centuries

The decision to attempt a run is ideally made by the batter who has the better view of the ball's progress, and this is communicated by calling: usually "yes", "no" or "wait". More than one run can be scored from a single hit: hits worth one to three runs are common, but the size of the field is such that it is usually difficult to run four or more. To compensate for this, hits that reach the boundary of the field are automatically awarded four runs if the ball touches the ground en route to the boundary or six runs if the ball clears the boundary without touching the ground within the boundary. In these cases the batters do not need to run. Hits for five are unusual and generally rely on the help of "overthrows" by a fielder returning the ball. If an odd number of runs is scored by the striker, the two batters have changed ends, and the one who was non-striker is now the striker. Only the striker can score individual runs, but all runs are added to the team's total.

Additional runs can be gained by the batting team as extras (called "sundries" in Australia) due to errors made by the fielding side. This is achieved in four ways: no-ball, a penalty of one extra conceded by the bowler if he breaks the rules; wide, a penalty of one extra conceded by the bowler if he bowls so that the ball is out of the batter's reach bye, an extra awarded if the batter misses the ball and it goes past the wicket-keeper and gives the batters time to run in the conventional way leg bye, as for a bye except that the ball has hit the batter's body, though not his bat. If the bowler has conceded a no-ball or a wide, his team incurs an additional penalty because that ball (i.e., delivery) has to be bowled again and hence the batting side has the opportunity to score more runs from this extra ball.

- Specialist roles

Captain (cricket) and Wicket-keeper

The captain is often the most experienced player in the team, certainly the most tactically astute, and can possess any of the main skillsets as a batter, a bowler or a wicket-keeper. Within the Laws, the captain has certain responsibilities in terms of nominating his players to the umpires before the match and ensuring that his players conduct themselves "within the spirit and traditions of the game as well as within the Laws".

The wicket-keeper (sometimes called simply the "keeper") is a specialist fielder subject to various rules within the Laws about his equipment and demeanour. He is the only member of the fielding side who can effect a stumping and is the only one permitted to wear gloves and external leg guards. Depending on their primary skills, the other ten players in the team tend to be classified as specialist batters or specialist bowlers. Generally, a team will include five or six specialist batters and four or five specialist bowlers, plus the wicket-keeper.

- Umpires and scorers

The game on the field is regulated by the two umpires, one of whom stands behind the wicket at the bowler's end, the other in a position called "square leg" which is about 15–20 metres away from the batter on strike and in line with the popping crease on which he is taking guard. The umpires have several responsibilities including adjudication on whether a ball has been correctly bowled (i.e., not a no-ball or a wide); when a run is scored; whether a batter is out (the fielding side must first appeal to the umpire, usually with the phrase "How's that?" or "Owzat?"); when intervals start and end; and the suitability of the pitch, field and weather for playing the game. The umpires are authorised to interrupt or even abandon a match due to circumstances likely to endanger the players, such as a damp pitch or deterioration of the light.

Off the field in televised matches, there is usually a third umpire who can make decisions on certain incidents with the aid of video evidence. The third umpire is mandatory under the playing conditions for Test and Limited Overs International matches played between two ICC full member countries. These matches also have a match referee whose job is to ensure that play is within the Laws and the spirit of the game.

The match details, including runs and dismissals, are recorded by two official scorers, one representing each team. The scorers are directed by the hand signals of an umpire . For example, the umpire raises a forefinger to signal that the batter is out (has been dismissed); he raises both arms above his head if the batter has hit the ball for six runs. The scorers are required by the Laws to record all runs scored, wickets taken and overs bowled; in practice, they also note significant amounts of additional data relating to the game.

A match's statistics are summarised on a scorecard. Prior to the popularisation of scorecards, most scoring was done by men sitting on vantage points cuttings notches on tally sticks and runs were originally called notches.According to Rowland Bowen, the earliest known scorecard templates were introduced in 1776 by T. Pratt of Sevenoaks and soon came into general use.It is believed that scorecards were printed and sold at Lord's for the first time in 1846.

- thank you for buy & read this book

have a great day of your
from : Mr Vivek Kumar Pandey

- This All Credit Goes To My Super Hero Daddy. “Always Love You dad’.

Printed by Libri Plureos GmbH in Hamburg,
Germany